WITHDRAWN

Teaching Beyond the Standards

18 Ideas with Work Options for Teachers, K–12

William R. Martin
with
Arvinder K. Johri

SCARECROWEDUCATION
Lanham, Maryland • Toronto • Oxford
2005

Published in the United States of America
by ScarecrowEducation
An imprint of The Rowman & Littlefield Publishing Group, Inc.
4501 Forbes Boulevard, Suite 200, Lanham, Maryland 20706
www.scarecroweducation.com

PO Box 317
Oxford
OX2 9RU, UK

British Library Cataloguing in Publication Information Available

Library of Congress Cataloging-in-Publication Data

Martin, William R. (William Reed), 1934–
   Teaching beyond the standards : 18 ideas with work options for teachers, K–12 /
William R. Martin, Arvinder K. Johri.
      p.   cm.
   Includes bibliographical references.
   ISBN 1-57886-223-X (pbk. : alk. paper)
   1. Effective teaching.   2. Awareness—Study and teaching.   3. Life skills—
Study and teaching.   I. Johri, Arvinder K., 1966–   II. Title.

LB1025.3.M3384 2005
371.102—dc22   2004022657

∞ ™ The paper used in this publication meets the minimum requirements of American
National Standard for Information Sciences—Permanence of Paper for Printed Library
Materials, ANSI/NISO Z39.48-1992. Manufactured in the United States of America.

For "Little E" and Lauren:

*May they continue to grow
in grace, strength, beauty, and wisdom!*

—William R. Martin

*To my daughter Apoorva,
who has shown me how
to "see" my students.*

—Arvinder K. Johri

CONTENTS

CONTENTS

PREFACE: A WORD ON STANDARDS

We love standards! Well, maybe that's a bit strong, but we do appreciate and respect them. And, we prefer to encourage teaching *beyond* the standards from a perspective that acknowledges and supports and complements what students should know and be able to do at different grade levels (i.e., academic standards). The current clamor for measurable content performance benchmarks arguably started with "A Nation at Risk," the 1983 national report that questioned our students' ability to compete in a global economy. Many politicians and some educators responded with a single mantra, *standards for every student*, and all states but Iowa, where standards are determined district by district, quickly developed standards for learning in the core areas of English, mathematics, science, history, and social science. Today, the standards initiative is emphasized by the federal No Child Left Behind Act signed by President George W. Bush in January 2001, which requires, for instance, all students to achieve 100% proficiency on state standards in mathematics and reading by the 2013–2014 school year. Proficiency checks, however, may vary. Nebraska, for example, has said "no" to mandatory statewide tests on curriculum standards. Rather, assessment there is done by school districts using portfolios to measure student progress. This illustrates the second general type of education standards: performance standards, or "how well" students must perform in order to meet the academic/content standards.

In our own professional experience, teachers are mostly agreeable to working with required national, state, and local standards and their assessments. As one of our very pragmatic colleagues puts it, "I love teaching because I love children, but I also want to be a good employee." (Here in Virginia, of course, we may be a bit influenced philosophically by Thomas Jefferson, who in his *Notes on the State of Virginia* [1781] perhaps anticipated one kind of standards by proposing a public school system in which "the best geniuses will be raked from the rubbish annually" [p. 94]!) More to the point, however, professional teachers everywhere understand that learning is a factual (and emotional) experience, with standards providing a major helping of the desired facts that educational leaders—often with political input—decide students should encounter in schools. Still, and this is the point of *Teaching Beyond the Standards*, student growth and development involve more than gaining particular sets of facts and learnings, such as those from the *Standards of Learning for Virginia Public Schools* (1995) for physical science: "The student will investigate and understand basic principles of electricity and magnetism" (p. 48). Or, those from the national K–8 standards determined by Mid-continent Research for Education and Learning (2003): A student in language arts should "understand specific devices an author uses to accomplish his or her purpose (persuasive techniques, style, portrayal of themes, language)" (p. 7). Students do not leave their *feelings* at the classroom door; how they grow emotionally with regard to subject matter (hate it, like it, fear it), and as maturing and responsible and capable people, is at least as important as how they achieve intellectually.

The major criticism of the standards movement from practicing teachers is that standards overly regulate what and how teachers teach. (For nonreflective teachers, this may especially be true.) Other common concerns include the following:

- Standards can seem like unwelcome commandments handed down from higher authorities. In Anne Arundel County, Maryland, for instance, teachers are asked to use daily curriculum pacing guides at every grade level and in almost every subject. (School district staff say the guides are not meant to inhibit teachers' instructional creativity, but rather to ensure that every child is exposed to a rigorous curriculum geared to state standards.)

- Standards stifle teacher flexibility and undermine student enthusiasm for learning.

- Standards take up too much academic learning time, and students are losing art and music opportunities, field trips, and the like as teachers focus instructional time on "teaching to the test."

- Standards vary (from state to state), and students lose consistency as they enter and leave state educational systems. In Colorado, for example, districts have the choice of adopting state standards or developing their own as long as they meet or exceed the state's expectations. So, a student leaving Colorado and entering a classroom in Virginia may well not be "up on" local standards that are developed by the commonwealth and that are consistent throughout Virginia.

- Standards require entirely new lesson plans, and teachers today don't have enough time or sufficiently high salaries compatible with this kind of effort.

- Standards, and their assessments, are not "fair" for special needs students (ESL, LD, "at risk").

- Standards from a variety of professional sources compete with state standards for instructional attention (e.g., TESOL, NCATE, NCTE, NCTM).

In common classroom practice, and along with stress, the negatives, and the high level of emotional feeling about standards, teachers have also come to understand that academic content standards and their assessment results can be quite useful. Standards provide a high-stakes measurement for teachers and students of student progress and needs (e.g., for graduation); provide a high academic "bar"—and students, and teachers, tend to live up to (high) expectations; serve as a core for specific lessons or units; help students understand *what* is expected and *when* in the academic component of their educational environment; help maintain connections and reinforcement in learning from grade to grade (vertical coordination) and across grades (horizontal coordination); and provide useful benchmarks against which teachers can evaluate their own accountability for student learning. In addition, teachers are recognizing that they are already meeting many required standards, and, with a little tweaking, existing lessons can be expanded to meet even more. In sum, teachers view standards as designed to provide minimums, with both schools and teachers normally encouraged to go *beyond* what is prescribed, a reality consistent with the intent of our book.

We argue that teaching beyond the standards (e.g., teaching positive self-concept) can provide students with a mental toughness for meeting initial success with standards assessments. Teaching effectively beyond the standards strengthens students' writing and calculating skills as they work with verbal communication skills and computer technology. Teaching students awareness, organization, and creative thinking allows students to more successfully attack the standards and their assessments. And, not to be forgotten, teaching beyond the standards can get the motivational juices—for teaching and learning of both students and teacher—flowing more strongly as part of enjoying the instructional process. Having and maintaining a sense of humor with standards contributes to working effectively with them. One student response we saw to the question "Explain one of the processes by which water can be made safe to drink" was "Filtration makes water safe to drink because it removes large pollutants like grit, sand, dead sheep and canoeists." A sense of humor can motivate teaching and learning as well as stimulate enjoyment of life in classrooms.

So, our word on standards is that we like them—and we say that from experience. Arvinder works with standards on a daily basis in her current job teaching sixth-, seventh-, and eighth-grade English. And Bill teaches student teachers and interns throughout northern Virginia how to teach successfully with standards in their K–12 classrooms. With our book, we are not in competition with standards. We do believe strongly that there is room in the classroom curriculum for more than standards and that the "more" can both supplement and complement the standards to be taught. Our book presents 18 ideas that enhance the development of students beyond the acquisition of facts and standards that may last only until related assessments are completed. We strongly believe that professional, reflective teachers with creativity, skill, a sense of humor, and commitment can effectively teach beyond the standards. Further, we believe that a substantial number of teachers *want* to teach beyond the standards— and should want to. Students deserve the best teachers have to offer, and for K–12 students that means working with them on more than academic content standards.

If you would like more on standards than this brief overview, an excellent comprehensive resource is the Association for Supervision and Curriculum Development (www.ascd.org), with material such as *Succeeding*

With Standards: Linking Curriculum, Assessment, and Action Planning by Judy F. Carr and Douglas E. Harris, 2001. The bottom line on standards, however, is to lay out what students should know; test them on it; and then hold the teachers and schools accountable for their scores. But now, we would like to get on with our ideas and work options for teaching *beyond* the standards.

ACKNOWLEDGMENTS

This last book of my professional career owes its existence in large measure to my wonderful wife, and best friend, Mary, who consistently and cheerfully and with great competence helped with the work of the manuscript—from idea through publication—and who, when all was done, accepted an autographed copy with a laugh!

I also wish to thank the administrators in the Graduate School of Education who were exceedingly professional in giving me time to work on the manuscript: Jeff Gorrell, Martin Ford, and Mark Gore. They are an especially fine group of faculty leaders.

Thanks also go to Arvinder's talented 14-year-old daughter, Apoorva, who developed the graphics that introduce the point of each of our 18 ideas from a student's perspective.

INTRODUCTION

Let's start at the very beginning, as said in one of our favorite plays, *The Sound of Music*, "a very good place to start." The beginning is the students. Without them, there is no need for the K–12 teaching–learning enterprise and its preoccupation with standards. Your students are the best their parents or guardians have to send. You may not be in initial agreement with parents that each child sent to you is special in some positive way, but as a professional teacher you need to act as though they are and that you are pleased to help them grow socially and emotionally, as well as academically.

That brings us to this little book written for practicing teachers and for students looking at teaching as a career. We applaud the standards movement and encourage the factual base it is providing to increase student knowledge and understanding. However, we think student growth involves getting into realms that not only enrich the standards but also go beyond them. It's teaching outside the (standards) box that we advocate. These realms that we have identified as interrelated ideas for teaching and learning beyond the standards are named in the contents. We suggest 18 important ideas that allow for attending to at least one idea during each two weeks of the typical instructional year, if such is your planning choice. Any way you decide to work with them, you will find each of the 18 ideas is organized with some underlying thoughts from us as to how the idea "plays out" in our thinking, followed by some work options for helping you, as a K–12 teacher, teach the idea in your classroom.

A few of the ideas and work options we include may be a bit unconventional for some readers. We intentionally did not include ideas on learning a second language, teaching globalism and peace education, providing art/music instruction, or teaching about religion in schools and classrooms. These topics may be more conventional to some readers, and they are beyond the standards and certainly worthy of attention, but they are well covered in other accessible texts. For sure, all of our 18 ideas can fit in any legitimate curriculum. If teachers have the will, they can eventually find the way! In addition, the 18 can be taught in any subject area; they are particularly geared to English/language arts, science, math, and social studies. They can be taught, with modifications, at all grade levels.

The ideas and their accompanying work options are written so that usually everyone will learn something from them. Mainly, the work options help further develop the ideas. Both the work options and their related ideas can be taught in city, suburban, or rural schools. They certainly can be taught in "pieces"—not all work options need to be done to get across the point of an idea, and not all students need necessarily be exposed to all of the options or all of the ideas. You know your students best; *you* choose what to teach and to whom when you work beyond the standards. In addition, the work options do not require expensive equipment or sophisticated technology. These can help, of course, but mainly what you need is time (which you can make, but it's not easy), energy (which you can produce), skill (which you have or can gain), and desire to teach these concepts (which, if you really want to help kids, should be on your instructional menu).

At the close of each idea and set of work options, we provide guide and follow-up questions for teachers and students to direct their action and interaction on the idea or its options in the classroom environment and for possible follow-up in or out of the school setting. These questions also help teach the idea. In both the work options and the guide and follow-up questions, we placed some appropriate references and sources for additional information. Our belief is like that of 18th-century British author and lexicographer Dr. Samuel Johnson, who argued that knowledge is of two kinds. We know a subject ourselves, or we know where we can find information about it.

The final section of our book provides a summary and conclusion for our view of teaching beyond the standards. We end with two fully developed sample lesson plans; one shows the *direct* teaching of one of the 18 ideas where the idea stands, independently, by itself in the lesson plan or curriculum, and the other shows one of the 18 ideas *merged* with teaching academic content standards. Both approaches work well in teaching beyond the standards.

Overall, we especially write for teachers who are flexible in their thinking about what should be going on in classrooms and are still at least somewhat idealistic and optimistic about what can be done to help students be what they can be. In our view, that includes complementing and supplementing today's emphasis on standards. Sources for our ideas and options are our own teaching and talks with teachers, our reflective and creative thinking and philosophy, our professional experiences and conferences, and our observations and readings and feelings. We *like* these 18 ideas and their related work options! We don't claim to present a book that is entirely new material but rather one that collects, combines, and organizes some of what is "out there"—one that is extremely pertinent to our belief in the importance of teaching beyond the standards to educate the "whole child."

As to other items of introduction, please note that we've written the book in a direct, informal, conversational style with a little invention and humor added in to increase readability. That works for us—and we hope for you. With you in mind who will read and use this book, we've merged into our ideas and work options the 1992 Interstate New Teacher Assessment and Support Consortium (INTASC) principles pertinent to current teacher education and ongoing professional development. In using the full power of the book for practice in elementary, middle school, and secondary classrooms or for discussion in college preservice courses, especially those with clinical experiences, we recommend keeping in mind the following guidelines:

- Teach beyond the standards when you are reasonably at ease with teaching *to* the standards. (But don't necessarily wait until you are finished with the standards. You will never get "finished.")

- Teach with attention to connections. The 18 ideas in this text, for instance, have many real connections to one another as well as to the standards. Students should be helped to see these connections and to understand that separations and divisions are made for instructional purposes (teacher emphasis) and logistical purposes (e.g., academic learning time available), not because the items are innately and uniquely separate from one another.

- Get continuous information on how your students are doing with regard to the standards. Are they scoring on assessment tests appropriate to their ability and learning experiences? That's your first priority. Teaching beyond the standards may well keep students interested overall, thereby helping you better teach the standards and helping them better achieve in assessment measures of the standards. The National Center for Education Statistics (2003) recently noted that over the past two decades, 12th graders have reported a declining interest in school. In 2000, only 28% said their school work was "often or always meaningful," down from the 40% who thought their classes were meaningful in 1983. Moreover, the center found that 5 out of every 100 young adults enrolled in high school in October 1999 left school before October 2000 without successfully completing a high school program. (Such a figure may have even more impact when compared with an automobile assembly line, where 5 cars out of 100 being unfinished when released into society would cause general public uproar.) Perhaps, then, *what* is being taught *is* a significant factor in student interest and subsequent retention in school.

- Work on your time management. With creative effort, you *will* be able to massage your required curriculum enough to find time for teaching beyond the standards. Team teaching might work. One team member could review standards for those who need the work; the other teacher could teach beyond the standards for the other students. (Remember, we are not arguing that you need to do one before starting the other or that all students need the same amount of everything; you can merge teaching beyond the standards *with* teaching to standards.) Include in your time management time for assessing and evaluating how you and the students are doing *and* how you both feel about what is going on beyond the standards.

- Add to your teaching skills repertoire. Through professional reading, continuing education courses, in-service workshops, professional conferences, and the like, locate and practice instructional skills that will assist you in motivating and teaching well—both the standards and beyond the standards. You are also likely to find more fulfillment in teaching as you gain skills. And as you become more "seasoned," you may be less likely to leave teaching, as do many of your colleagues; almost half are gone by the end of their fifth year of teaching.

- Keep your "significant others" informed—in advance, if possible. (Sometimes you may have a "teachable moment" and no advance information can be provided. In these cases, use a follow-up memo or letter home or other procedure.) Information can be provided informally and given a lower profile than the academic feedback or feedforward, but it is wise to let principals and parents know you are teaching beyond the standards.

- Enlist on a continuing basis both volunteer students and parents to help with the preparation, teaching, and evaluation of work done with the 18 ideas. Be sure to evaluate those helping so you know whether to extend their help or decrease/eliminate it with thanks.

- Remember to invest teaching beyond the standards with your own thinking and energy. We offer a start in this book with enough detail so you can work with the 18 ideas and their options immediately. We invite you to revise, modify, add, and continue on from what we have provided. You should find that the work options are enjoyable to teach, provide variety in instruction, and are interesting for you and the students. They are there to help you teach the idea to which they are connected.

So, that's it. *Teaching Beyond the Standards* is a relatively short, very practical book centered on teaching to the whole child, with the purpose of making that kind of teaching more convenient for teachers. Learning, after all, is a factual *and* emotional experience. Many students may be turned off by instruction to standards and turned on by teaching beyond the standards (or the reverse may be true). Some students may be quite happy with both learning to meet standards and learning beyond the standards. Some students may be unhappy with both. Teacher caring, intelligence, concern, creativity, flexibility, specific skill, and general competence are always crucial in the difficult endeavor of helping students learn. What we offer is a book to help them in the "beyond standards" part of the learning process.

In sum, our book offers clearly stated ideas and work options. Our suggestion is to work with one (or more) of the 18 ideas over each two-week period during an instructional year. There are sufficient options for this to happen efficiently in your classes, especially with the addition of your own creative thinking and energy to our generic and somewhat skeletal outlines. Our options are offered for use in a typical classroom, and most can be brought into play without needing special facilities or equipment or any serious cost. You are always invited to add both your own ideas and options. If you are currently teaching, you are invited to adopt or adapt the information presented to make it more meaningful for *your* students. You may choose to move a certain option from where we placed it to a different idea. That's fine. The ideas and options are all connected and interlinked anyway and are separated mainly for organizational purposes. In that way, you can also better decide if you prefer to teach an idea or an option by itself, or if you would rather merge something from *Teaching Beyond the Standards* with your regular curriculum.

As a last point of introduction, we believe that in working with our book, you will likely increase your own enjoyment in teaching. And that's a good thing! As we've worked with practicing teachers and students in preservice courses with field experience, we've found that they are committed to teaching what needs to be taught; they spend a great deal of academic learning time on standards, but they also want to—and like to—do more (teaching beyond the standards) for their students' enjoyment and learning and their own. So, we invite you now into the process with the help of *Teaching Beyond the Standards*.

IDEA ONE
TEACHING AWARENESS AND ORGANIZATION

Teachers regularly teach English/language arts, math, science, and social studies. They should also teach awareness and organization in the classroom. If students are to achieve success in the former, they need to have a well-developed understanding of where they "are" in time and space, the key to conscious awareness and organization: "How much time do I have to complete this test?" (time in the *here and now*); "How long do I have with my cooperative learning group today?"; "How long am I going to listen to the teacher before my attention turns to the game?"; "Is my homework due tomorrow or at the end of the week?" (*future* time); "Is the current arrangement of furniture in my classroom conducive to my learning, or is the spacing more set up to encourage my 'goofing off'?" (external space); "As I get ready to leave today's class, do I realize that I am being approached from behind by an 'enemy' or a friend, and how do I feel about that likely intrusion into my personal protective bubble?" (internal space). The instructional concept of providing "alone time" serves as an example of how both awareness and organization are rooted in time and space. Students are provided with 7 to 11 minutes (an odd number seems to increase the sense of importance and productivity) once or more each week to be *by themselves*—without a teacher or other students in close proximity—in order to reflect on what is going on in class and what role they play, or should play, in the unfolding events of the classroom. The students' situation can be perceived as analogous to an old tale from India that speaks to awareness and organization:

1

The Blind Men and the Elephant

Long ago in India, six blind men lived together. All of them had heard of elephants but had never "seen" one. Though they were blind they traveled to the Rajah's palace to acquaint themselves with an elephant. In the courtyard each of them touched a different part of the huge animal, and each came away with a different impression:

An elephant is like a wall. (his side)
An elephant is round like a snake. (his trunk)
An elephant is sharp like a spear. (his tusk)
An elephant is like a tree. (his leg)
An elephant is like a fan. (his ear)
An elephant is like a rope. (his tail)

They could not agree on a description of the animal and argued out of control. The Rajah overheard and explained to them that each touched only a part, but all parts had to be put together for a true expression. The blind men decided that each of them had a different perception and "to find out the whole truth we must put all the parts together."

During their alone time, students think about their individual impressions of classroom life and their own contributions to its effectiveness. A teacher-led whole-class debriefing could follow alone time to describe the "whole elephant"—to look at the whole class at *this* point in time—and give the class and its individual members a renewed sense of purpose and direction. Teaching awareness and organization through alone time is part of how *the teacher understands how students differ in their approaches to learning and creates instructional opportunities that are adapted to diverse learners* (INTASC principle 3).

Methods and intent to bring about learning in awareness and organization for all students should be at least equal to what is used with teaching to the standards. It should not be taken for granted that students are aware and organized. Some, of course, will be more so than others. Teachers who directly teach awareness and organization establish routines themselves that students must learn and follow, such as using advance organizers to help students link what they know to new information; or asking students where they can find items in the classroom, such as markers and paper needed for the learning centers or for their portfolios; or identifying for students and maintaining a "no interrupting table," where private conferences are held with individual children. Another routine involves asking students to take a pencil from a can of clearly visible pre-sharpened pencils instead of disturbing instruction with "I can't find my pencil," then requiring them to show their own sharp pencils to the teacher before the next class. Precise and clear teacher directions for using learning centers and doing assignments also facilitate the learning of awareness and organization, as does holding students to good study habits such as setting realistic goals, focusing on main ideas, taking notes, looking for links between what's being taught and previous learning, and asking questions to assist in summarizing learning. The use of student journals is another way to help students be more aware and organized. Students write down their own thoughts (awareness) and do so in at least three sentences every Monday, Wednesday, and Friday (organization).

When teaching awareness and organization, teachers structure their students' learning environment so that students find a comfort zone, *what students can control or change for a realistic chance of academic success*, within which organization for continued learning is done on the basis of prior and growing personal competence. In this comfort zone where academics are "not so hard," students see self-empowerment for academic risk taking "now" or "later" as possible, if not exciting, and as something that can spring from a strong platform of personal organization. In addition, they come to a fuller awareness of their own learning style, *how their minds operate for learning and how they adapt to their environments.* Are they visual/spatial learners, kinesthetic learners, or auditory learners? Are they field dependent (global, "big picture" learners) or field independent (analytical, detail-focused learners)? Is their learning mostly connected to inter- or intrapersonal or musical or naturalistic or linguistic or logical/mathematical intelligence? Is their learning style some combination of these or others? Within the comfort zone, students should be allowed time to organize and carry out their learning in line with their dominant style(s) while being given opportunities to reach out beyond those styles to learn new things in new ways from different people in a variety of circumstances. They become increasingly aware, organized, *adaptive* learners.

In sum, the teaching of awareness and organization can be done within the teaching of standards and the regular curriculum (reminding students of study skills), or it can be done as separate, independent lessons (teaching students their learning styles). Regardless of the teacher's choice of approach, teaching awareness and organization based on a developing sense of time and space needs to be consistently united with ongoing academic instruction and with continuing reflection, analysis, and evaluation. It is through awareness and organization that achievement with the standards and academic life in general is well met and students are helped to become responsible and mature adults.

Work Options

Self-Awareness Through Reading

Ask students to bring to each class a book chosen by them (approval from parents or guardians is a good idea). Have books in the classroom, as well. (Each classroom should possess a minimum of seven books per student, according to the International Reading Association). Provide students with alone time at the start of the class period or at another appropriate time in class to read. These books, fiction or nonfiction, may well increase their awareness of their own emotional range. They may achieve a "felt emotional knowledge" from the book. In the excellent adolescent novel *The Pigman* by Paul Zindel (1983), for instance, one of the book's main characters (John) comes to accept the sobering and very personal reality of thoughtless actions and the impact of a friend's death when he says, "There was no one else to blame anymore . . . no place to hide. . . . Our life would be what we made of it—nothing more, nothing less" (p. 149).

Study Skills and Tools

Provide lessons on study skills. For example, teach students that taking good notes is *not* writing down everything the teacher says. And that keeping ready-to-go materials at one's desk—maybe in a small container attached to the desk by Velcro—can make for more efficient use of work time. Also, "cool" tools such as Time Trackers at student desks can help them keep on time. These plastic visual timers/clocks are available from Learning Resources at www.learningresources.com. Students could also be taught to occasionally make and use simple two-dimensional scales (see figure 1.1). On these, they plot their awareness of how they solve problems or complete tasks while dealing with people. In two-dimensional plotting, for example, a "9 × 1" is all about "task," with "people" concerns being ignored. A theoretical "9 × 9" means the task is perfectly completed and the people involved are totally satisfied.

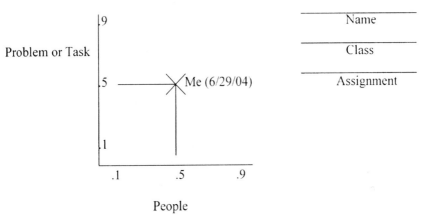

Figure 1.1   The 2-D Scale

The Johari Window

Teach students to use the Johari window to increase personal awareness and growth (see figure 1.2). The window allows students to explore themselves and discover new things about themselves, including abilities.

	Known to self	Not known to self
Known to others	1. Area of common knowledge	2. Blind area (things my friends haven't told me about yet, such as bad breath)
Not known to others	3. Hidden or avoided area (my secrets and things I haven't had a chance to tell yet)	4. Hidden potential area (things I never dreamed I could do or be)

Figure 1.2   The Johari Window

The window does not imply indiscriminate openness; there are things about each individual that aren't relevant to the business of the classroom. However, as the "hidden potential" quadrant decreases (a change in any one quadrant will affect all other quadrants), "new" abilities are likely to come into personal and/or common awareness.

Alone-Time Activities

Integrate alone-time activities within the regular curriculum in the first weeks of school to help students become comfortable, if not more self-organized, in the academic environment. In the elementary grades some activities include designing "I" collages using words, pictures, and symbols clipped from magazines; making shape or season identifications followed by a journal entry elaborating the reasons for the identification; using a personal thumbprint to create an animal that represents the student; creating drawings or lists of personal talents; and drawing self-portraits using different mediums. Students can sketch self-portraits based on how they think they are perceived by their peers and on how they perceive themselves. Writing letters of introduction and creating mnemonic representations of their strengths are some other ways to help students enjoy alone time and perhaps build their own self-awareness through acknowledging, sharing and celebrating their distinctive individuality.

Taking a Reflective Stance

Have students implement self-reflection strategies to help them become more reflective learners oriented toward improving their ability to organize. Students can create verbal or artistic metaphors of their learning styles after a teacher-led lesson on multiple intelligences and their real-world applications. They can maintain a two-column learning log, detailing factual and key information in one column and reflections and questions in response to class information in the other column. For young children, the teacher can compile a collection of picture books with examples of organization (illustrated alphabet books) to initiate or build the process of personal organization. Students can discuss these picture books from different perspectives and explore questions that encourage their own sense of organization (e.g., "Does Spanish have more alphabet letters than English does?").

Visualizing the "Big Picture"

Ask students to set goals to improve their sense of organization. Students often are quite adept at plugging in the small pieces but often have no grasp of the "big picture" in an instructional sequence. Setting goals provides them with a sense of direction and adds the essential element of accountability for day-to-day decisions. Teaching students to set short- and long-term goals based on a realistic analysis of their time and responsibilities and to prioritize those goals based on where they want to be at a critical time (end of a unit of instruction) is a critical step in learning to organize more effectively and efficiently. Students can maintain interactive journals with a division that lists individual goals, their subparts, a timeline, and evaluation criteria spanning a grading period on the right side and day-to-day entries, responses, reflections, teacher comments, and a look ahead into the next day on the left side of the journal.

Self-Organizing Strategies

Have students keep a calendar, maintain assignment notebooks, and/or create a daily to-do list or study list. A calendar organizer can serve multiple functions: as a timeline for a project, as a record-keeping device for due dates for short- and long-term projects, and as a reflection-for-the-day log. Asking students to fill out a daily review form reflecting on the day's learning, stumbling blocks, and successes not only reinforces the day's learning but also sets the framework for the next day. Daily review of notes, making a test-prep checklist, checking rubrics to evaluate the completion of assignments, maintaining editing/proofreading checklists, making flashcards, and using mnemonic devices to recall essential information are a few self-organizing strategies that can help students actively develop their organizing skills and consequently improve their own classroom performance.

Organizing Information

Teach graphic organizers (such as cluster webs, mind maps, compare and contrast Venn diagrams, cause/effect organizers, timelines, sensory charts) (see figure 1.3).

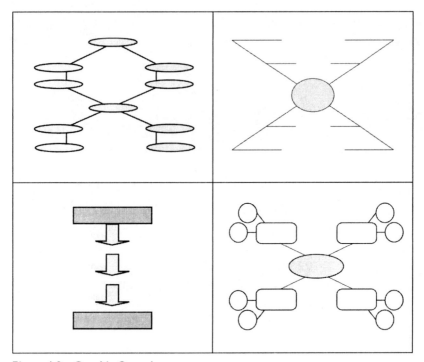

Figure 1.3   Graphic Organizers

These are excellent springboards for helping students organize information as well as their thinking about the information. Graphic organizers visually demonstrate relationships, break down complex concepts into structured units, translate abstract concepts into concrete classifications, and redirect focus on key concepts. They help students "see" key facts and understand underlying patterns. Graphic organizers enhance creative thinking and provide clues about information received—from the text, for instance. The website teachers.teach-nology.com/web_tools/graphic_org offers concept webs, KWL charts, SQ3R charts, timelines, and Venn diagrams. Inspiration Version 7 software, designed for grades 6 to 12, helps students and teachers develop ideas; organize concepts into webs, graphs, diagrams, and outlines; and analyze complex topics. Mind mapping is well presented in Joyce Wycoff's book *Mindmapping: Your Personal Guide to Exploring Creativity and Problem-Solving* (1991).

Enlarging Personal Space

Encourage students to admit differences and accept multiple points of view, which can enhance their personal space to include an enlarged comfort zone for tolerance of others. Students can participate in multicultural workshops facilitating intergroup dialogue, write and share personal narratives on experiences with prejudice or bias, have fishbowl discussions on gender differences and stereotypes, and create gender identity posters. They can list incidents in which they felt included in, or excluded from, the learning process and role-play controversial issues surrounding race, gender, and heterosexuality. E-pal projects (web-based collaborative interactions) cultivate intercultural relationships; foster appreciation for diverse cultures; and help students discover meeting points in diversity with students across racial, cultural, and geographical boundaries. Teachers can access activity booklets appropriate for middle and upper grades and obtain a free copy of "Reaching Across Boundaries: Talk to Create Change" (grades 7 to 12) by logging on to www.mixitup.org/teachers.

Guide and Follow-Up Questions for Teachers and Students

1. Am I, as an aware teacher, keeping up to date on materials that can help me help students become continually more aware and organized? For instance, time is always a concern for teaching awareness and organization. Do I refer to books such as *Time to Teach, Time to Learn* by Chip Wood (1999)? This one especially helps teachers, K–8, who want to change how they use time in order to transform classrooms into democratic communities of learning where teaching beyond the standards is part of the day's work.

2. Do I show a strong sense of awareness and organization myself? For instance, do I check my sight lines so I can see all my students? Do I write myself Post-it notes with key phrases for conducting small group instruction? Do I monitor academic learning time so that I leave time for closure at the end of the lesson? Do I adjust "on the fly" so I am not trying to do too much and yet maintain an appropriate pace?

3. Do the students and I work together on specifics connected to the teaching of awareness and organization, such as specifics for effective time management: setting an agenda, assessing and evaluating our current use of time, clarifying objectives, estimating how long assignments will take, setting priorities and doing things in order of importance, planning the best use of our time for meeting our objectives, eliminating time wasters, and monitoring our use of time on an ongoing basis? Do we work proactively and as needed on organizational skills such as sequencing, sorting, comparing, contrasting, and alphabetizing? Do we acknowledge the importance of peripheral vision and maybe even practice it in class (e.g., seeing what a neighbor is up to while typing on personal computers or, with middle school students, discussing the studied awareness and subsequent interaction, or lack thereof, between boys and girls at the school dance)?

4. As a teacher, am I an organized and reflective learner? Do I usually set some time aside to recap the day and reflect on the day's events?

5. As a student, do I keep a to-do list that indicates high-, medium-, and low-priority tasks? Can I rearrange priorities based on changing demands? Do I create a schedule for each week that includes sufficient advance time for important deadlines and projects? Can I figure backward from a deadline to estimate how much time each step in the process will take? Do I make frequent checks on how daily tasks relate to long-term goals?

6. Are my students aware of the study strategies used by their well-organized and academically strong classmates? Do I give them opportunities for exchanging this information? Are they aware of their possible misconceptions about certain study strategies, such as allocating nearly the same time for reviewing each content area (the ones they "know" and the ones they "don't know") and not setting priorities? (Students need to be able to identify high-priority and low-priority tasks and pace out their tasks strategically but not necessarily uniformly.)

7. Might it be useful for me to visit the interactive website

www.educate.com/discovery/discovery.cfm to discover the strengths and struggles of students in different content areas and skills and to compare the feedback with students' perceptions of their own strengths and weaknesses? Developed by the Sylvan Learning Center, the site is free and offers information on both the value of organizing—and its lack—in learning. The feedback is available in a performance graph format or a performance analysis synopsis.

TEACHING HOW TO COPE WITH CHANGE AND STRESS

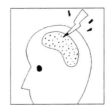

Change is the one constant students encounter in their journey through school. Over 2,500 years ago, Greek philosopher Heraclitus stated, "There is nothing permanent except change." For example, ESL students frequently experience change (and stress) during their period of acculturation. They are frequently caught between the culture and ways of their parents and the culture and customs of their new environment. Many have left difficult or dangerous situations and endured extreme hardships, both physical and mental, in their journeys to U.S. schools—where they encounter even more change when learning to use English properly. But all students, K–12, not just ESL teenagers, live immersed in change, and more is coming at them all the time and at an accelerated pace. From the invention of electricity to its mass use, for example, 46 years elapsed; from the invention of the World Wide Web to its mass use, 7 years!

From helping students reflect on the terrorist attacks of September 11, 2001, to the changing alerts of today that affect school and society; from helping confused teenagers to calming children frightened by divorce or burdened by demands of new homework; from helping students learn English to helping them deal with change and stress in taking AP courses or worrying about college admissions; from helping students deal with old interpersonal conflicts to helping them mesh with new partners for demanding assignments, teachers are confronted with realistic reasons for teaching how to cope with change and stress. One teacher with whom we worked wrote in his journal: "Talked with a couple of kids yesterday who realized they were not going to pass for the year. Some just stopped coming to class. I found out about those who had stopped coming. They were some really smart kids. I saw one of them at 7-Eleven with an older group of guys buying beer. It really bugs me that these kids were not reached. Something happened in their lives that led them to this choice. Was it something in the school? At home? Could we as teachers have helped them better deal with their problems early on? Reminds me of what my favorite old Pittsburgh Pirates pitcher Vernon Law once said, 'Experience is a hard teacher because she gives the test first, the lesson afterward.'"

When teaching students how to cope with change, teachers might start by keeping in mind themselves that change often conflicts with the natural process of homeostasis, the body's efforts in self-regulation for maintaining equilibrium (balance). As biological organisms, our bodies try to compensate in heart rate, blood pressure, and respiration for disturbances and to maintain a steady state in the face of change. Knowing that physiological coping is in place, however, does not necessarily make it any easier to deal with students enmeshed emotionally and intellectually in the change process. Change with regard to emotions and academics comes in four categories, each of which might provide a kind of disturbance: knowledge change, attitude change, individual behavior change, and change in group performance. (There is also, for students, the reality of change in the organization in which they are embedded, like a new teacher taking over after the school year has already started. For this kind of change, consider looking into change theory, communications theory, and/or organizational theory.)

In teaching about the process of change in its different categories so that students can become better able to cope with it, teachers should choose to help students learn how new ideas get put into practice. First is the awareness stage at which students simply know about the new idea or emotion they encounter in the classroom or school. Second is the interest stage where the student is intrigued enough to seek more information. Third is the evaluation stage where, with facts in hand, the student runs a mental trial: "Can I really do this?" or "How can I do this?" Fourth is the trial stage where, if the student makes the decision to give the new idea a try, he or she lets it "play out" on at least a small scale. Fifth is the adoption stage; during this stage, the student is relatively satisfied with the new idea or emotion and puts it to use on a repeated basis. This we call learning, and it is a product of change and often the (good) stress that accompanies it.

Stress is broadly defined as the nonspecific response of the body to any demand made on it. According to Dr. Hans Selye (1974), a Canadian endocrinologist long considered the father of stress research, our initial response to any kind of stress is alarm, followed by resistance when the body repairs damage caused from the stress, and then exhaustion if the alarm or threat is continued over a long period of time. The effect of stress is determined in part by this duration and also by the intensity of the stressor and the student's external and internal environment: what has gone before, how close emotionally or physically students are to events that happen (stress can be self-imposed), how much the students are directly affected, and how they individually perceive the potentially stressful situation. Stress is further complicated by students' recognition of their ability to do something about it, which includes contemplating the following: Does it present a conflict in values? Is it a real threat to their wellbeing? Does it present a challenge seemingly beyond their resources for responding?

Stress is often an outcome of change; the two are closely related—change being a major cause of stress, and stress giving rise to dissatisfaction and thus becoming a motivating factor for change. Things may change by being "over," with the stress factors reduced, or a change in an event (an anniversary) may stir up new stress. Or, the feelings about a particular stressor may change over time. Even the same event can cause stress at one time and not at another. Stress comes in two forms: chronic and acute. Chronic stress is caused by constant emotional pressure the student can't readily control. It produces hormones that can weaken the immune system and increase student susceptibility to disease; it can contribute to the development of ulcers and headaches; it can underlie emotional and behavioral problems. Acute stress, on the other hand, is a response to imminent danger. It turbocharges the immune system with powerful hormones and prepares the body for fight or flight. Both of these forms of stress can impact on student energy and readiness for effective classroom performance.

Stressful events or conditions themselves (a high grade anticipated but not yet received) may also be pleasant and cause productive stress (eustress—from the Greek meaning "good") that keeps students alert and lively and jolts them out of boredom. Homework deadlines or a certain amount of time pressure, for example, may encourage productivity and efficiency. Distress, on the other hand, can be unpleasant and harmful. It is the kind of sensation experienced when a student is faced with too much paperwork or encounters an overload in classes. Overall, stress can not be avoided, nor should it be. It can be embraced as the spice of life, but it must be kept at a proper level, one particularly away from continual chronic distress. Teacher emphasis when dealing with stress must not be on elimination but on management.

Teachers who do attend to management, to teaching coping skills for change and stress, continually watch for student nonverbal behaviors such as facial expressions that show anger or sadness as well as excessive fidgeting or squirming. These can indicate a level of stress in the classroom that needs attention. In addition, they look for students who are continually tense, who show erratic performance, who have difficulty concentrating, or who are generally irritable. There are a variety of signs and symptoms of stress. For better or worse, stress is an undeniable fact of school life. It makes good sense, therefore, for teachers to teach coping skills. Teachers today who teach students how to cope effectively with change and stress give students a piece of the action; they sublet to students some ownership through coplanning and inventing learning options for what goes on in the classroom. (Telling is not teaching, and told is not taught when it comes to teaching coping skills or other learning.) As the president of Harvard, Lawrence Summers, is said to have remarked, "In the history of the world, no one has ever washed a rented car." If students get a real voice, some ownership, in how things are run, they will have opportunity to turn possible distress (e.g., about an assignment) into productive stress (the pressure is "on" because it is a teacher–student developed assignment that students want to do), with the brain signaling the adrenal glands to release hormones, including adrenaline, and the nerve cells to release norepinephrine. These powerful chemicals make the senses sharper, the muscles tighter, the heart pound faster, and the bloodstream fill with sugar for ready energy. The result can be a better, at least in the short term, accomplishment—a bout of precurtain jitters motivating a spectacular performance in the school play.

Teachers who teach management also have students systematically maintain portfolios that contain criteria revealing drafts of earlier work, thereby allowing students, teachers, and parents to observe change (e.g., in writing ability). Teachers who teach coping with change and stress do so for usually a short amount of time in any one session, maybe 40 minutes or so at most. (Emotions can run high with some topics and make learning more difficult.) And, they announce in advance what will be covered and discuss emerging feelings about the topic(s) in the course of the teaching without denying the legitimacy of the students' feelings. Teachers who teach coping skills anticipate. With ESL students, for example, they make native language dictionaries available in the classroom or advise students to bring a tape recorder to tape lectures so they can replay them later. They also create a respectful and well-organized workplace where language minority students are willing to suspend distress and take risks in front of native speakers.

When teaching how to cope with change and stress, teachers include the topic of stress management in their curriculum and concentrate on helping youngsters develop effective coping mechanisms that signify healthy adjustment to the realities of (classroom) life. They help students recognize and come to grips with questions such as the following: Do I attempt to connect with my stress, allowing me to better identify its roots and determine what needs to be changed? How much control do I have over the event causing me stress? Is the stressing event worth my time and attention; are the benefits greater than the energy I will have to expend? Is attempting to deal with the stress causing me more stress than the stressing event itself? Do I have a buddy or some kind of support system in the class with whom I can talk about my worries or where I can express my feelings? Do I know how to express irritation, and appreciation, to others? Am I flexible; can I give in once in a while? Do I set priorities and take one thing at a time? Do I do something for others and not concentrate so much on myself and my own situation? Do I try to predict and anticipate what might cause me stress? Do I trust my intuition but also realistically check out potential stressors? Do I know some mental exercises to help me cope with distress (e.g., concentrate on relaxing successive sets of muscles from the tips of my toes to the muscles in my forehead and neck)? Am I aware of my personal limits for moving from acceptable, benign stress to malignant distress? Do I use humor as a tension release? Can I take time off from a stress-producing project and detach myself from it (and maybe play around a little with something else that's pleasurable for me) without feeling guilty about it? Can I organize myself and my work in advance so stress does not build up unnecessarily (e.g., plan my "attack" on the task before I start it—break the large assignment into small parts to do and not procrastinate on doing them; delegate some of the work to others, if appropriate)? Do I set realistic goals for myself and then work on accomplishing them? Do I take action on changing/reducing stressors that I can change and develop tolerance for or change my attitude about the rest? Do I have and maintain a repertoire of strategies for dealing with stress, such as a win–win conflict resolution strategy? Am I willing to identify and work with and build on what I could accept out of the stress I encounter (an idea opposed to mine, yet one that has a kind of appeal for me)? For all students in their care, teachers who teach how to cope with change and stress are calming and usually straightforward and direct. They are both compassionate and authoritative, reassuring yet realistic. They respect students' intelligence and avoid false assurances. Overall, they help students understand that being fearful of change and being under stress are inevitable parts of life; it is normal, reasonable, and okay.

To close our thoughts on this idea for teaching how to cope with change and stress, we share the thought of historian Arnold Toynbee, in his *A Study of History* (1972), who held the basic premise that nations and people thrive only when they are contending with crises or challenges. We believe that to help students thrive in permeating school crises and with the never-ending challenges of classroom change and stress, INTASC principle 2 must come into play: *The teacher understands how children learn and develop and can provide learning opportunities that support their intellectual, social, and personal development.* Through a "cope-ability" emphasis within this framework, teachers can deepen the self-governing capacity of students and thereby help them coexist with, and perhaps lead, the constant, permeating, and sometimes roaring current of change and stress that can both challenge their lives and fulfill them.

Work Options

Portfolios

Although there are many types of portfolios, they share common writing drafts and samples, solutions to mathematics problems, projects, pieces of artwork, science charts, multimedia presentations, and similar artifacts important to the learner and presented in one coherent and colorful collection maintained over time (e.g., a grading period, a semester, a year). Portfolios are usually keyed to a teacher–student agreed-upon instructional purpose and ongoing assessment system, including a (flexible) time line. Their overall purpose is to allow the student to demonstrate his or her skills, efforts, and accomplishments—and to provide evidence of academic growth (change). In using the portfolio strategy, encourage your students to use technology to create and manage the portfolio. Remember to include assessment features such as teacher evaluations, results of progress conferences, results of peer swaps, rubrics, and student self-evaluations and reflections.

Scrapbooks

Ask students to write a personal true story in which they experienced stress or change. They could write about how they felt, what they saw or heard, and what they did. Have them include some "pleasant memory" stories coming out of a stressful situation or a major change they faced. Collect the stories and place them in a scrapbook that could be maintained in class. Be sure that students give written permission for their stories to be shared in the public arena of the classroom. The scrapbook becomes a vehicle for future reference and discussion about change and stress—and a means of creating empathy among class members for one another.

Measuring Stress and Evaluating Coping Skills

Have students make a ruler to measure their stress: "1" means "I am not upset at all," "12" means "I'm really, really upset," and "6" means "I'm pretty upset." "Rulers" can be turned in so you can assess where your students stand with regard to current stress on this project, assignment, or test or at this time of the year. Ask students to also make an accompanying personal coping skills chart. This starts by listing "The three things that give me the most stress are . . ." and "My symptoms of stress are . . ."; then it has two headings: Positive Ways I Cope With Stress (e.g., "I have and follow a normal routine in school") and Negative Ways I Cope With Stress (e.g., "I easily let my anger rule my on-task productivity and interfere with my interactions with others"). This chart and the "ruler" could be used in productive one-to-one conferences with the student(s) to improve learning. Remember, no one stress level is right for everyone; tolerance and acceptance for stress are built gradually.

Discovering Examples

Invite students to discover examples of change in fact or legend—perhaps in your, or their, favorite subject area. These can be shared in class. An example: In the 1500s, most people got married in June supposedly because they took their yearly bath in May and still smelled pretty good by June. However, they were starting to smell, so brides carried a bouquet of flowers to hide the body odor; from this story perhaps came our current custom of carrying a bouquet when getting married. The custom remains today about the flowers, but, hopefully, people take baths more often! Another and more "academic" example in world history: On March 31, 1854, two governments with conflicting goals found a way to sign an agreement without bloodshed—the Treaty of Kanagawa. The U.S. government was determined to take the lead in bringing Japan's two-century-old policy of self-imposed isolation to a close. The Fillmore administration sent Commodore Matthew C. Perry and a small fleet of sloops and the latest steam-powered ships to Tokyo Bay to insist on a treaty that would protect the rights of American whalers, provide for coaling ports, and eventually lead to trade. What began as a treaty of friendship imposed by threat of force (stress for all involved) became the foundation for great change in Japan as a nation and eventually for one of the world's most important bilateral relationships. Here's an interesting example in science: In the 1500s, people with money had plates made of pewter. Food with high acid content caused some of the lead to leak into the food, causing lead poisoning and even death. This happened most often with tomatoes, so for the next 400 years or so, tomatoes were considered poisonous. That has changed today, as teenage pizza eaters well know.

Mock Trials

Conduct mock trials with your students. You will need short scripts for your volunteer "bailiff," "judge," "defendant's attorney," "plaintiff's attorney," "jurors," "jury foreperson," "defendant," "plaintiff," and "witnesses." One way to get scripts is to write them, or ask students to write them with your advice and consent, using familiar stories for content such as "the big bad wolf versus the three little pigs" or "the trial of Hansel and Gretel." Mock trials tend to direct the classroom into becoming a community of discursive inquiry in which stress is likely to be accepted and perhaps better understood on a personal and group basis—and even enjoyed.

Classroom Library

Build a classroom library where students can read good books dealing with change and stress. One example is *A Death in the Family* by James Agee (2000); this book deals with the impact of a father's death on the members of his family—primarily his young son. Another example is *Of Mice and Men* by John Steinbeck (2002); it explores the nature of friendship in the relationship between two migrant workers. In *To Kill a Mockingbird* by Harper Lee (2002), a young brother and sister discover that their own father is the wisest, bravest man they know as he takes a stand against racial prejudice in a southern town. These and other "quality reads" are probably available in the school library if you don't have them in a classroom reading area.

Changing the Curriculum

Give students a dose of learning that's a change from the regular curriculum. Use, for example, the CIRCUSWORKS website, www.circus works.com, developed by Ringling Bros. and Barnum & Bailey. This site creatively connects the magic of the circus with curriculum for early elementary through middle school students and teachers. Nearly two dozen lesson plans are available. Lessons use a circus theme to engage students while simultaneously teaching them important science, math, and history skills with potentially less stressful results. Additional resources include a glossary of circus terms, games, puzzles, and coloring sheets as well as a suggested reading list.

Selected Activities for Coping With Change

Have students perform activities that make them more comfortable with change. One such activity is the "scenario," or "future history." In this activity, students string together one or more events (in science, math, writing and language study, or history) that might occur in the future. (Example in science: human exploration of Mars.) They make their convincing case for the probability of occurrence of the event(s). (The future is not predetermined, and there are preferable futures as well as probable ones.) The scenario is basically a narrative written from the point of view of a specific future date, such as 50 or 100 years hence. It also describes the logical and accurate sequence of events that occurred from the present leading up to that date and gives students practice in assessing the consequences of courses of action and decisions made in the past and present. Another activity is "individual forecasting," which invites the student to probe and describe possible upcoming change (related to an academic field) mainly through his or her own vision and intuition. (Example in social studies: "I predict a female will be president of the United States within 12 years.") The forecasting is done in short descriptive statements with probabilities, based on prior and current study, attached to them. In addition, the likelihood of occurrence of one development, as predicted, can be commented on in terms of its potential for increasing or decreasing the probability of occurrence of other developments. Both the "future histories" and the "individual forecasts" can be discussed in class in terms of the reality and rate of change itself, and perhaps in terms of the opportunity for individuals today to gain a greater feeling of control over their own personal futures.

Conflict Resolution Techniques

Reinforce the reality that stress connects closely to conflict, and conflict, like stress, is an inevitable part of everyday life. In the Christian Bible, for instance, Jesus says: "Do not think that I have come to bring peace on earth; I have not come to bring peace, but a sword" (Matthew 10:34). So, teach students some conflict resolution techniques for use in and out of class as individuals and in groups. For example, try role reversal where a student in conflict with another plays himself or herself, with a volunteer playing the role of the involved other (no names are used). The students enact the situation. From time to time, the students reverse roles. The student with the conflict that initiated the role reversal activity is confronted with a stimulus to think about why the "other" is doing what he or she is doing and can begin to view the situation from the viewpoint of the other person involved in the original conflict.

Another strong conflict resolution technique is mediating. It is a way of helping two or more students work out their differences in the presence of an observer (teacher or trained student) who keeps everything "fair." It takes time, but it works. What also works is verbal judo, which is derived from martial arts, referring to the use of a system against itself to avoid or cope with conflict and bring about desired change. Following are the basic principles of verbal judo: Learn the structure of the system being dealt with (classroom grading system, group work system, school testing system, home/parent requirements, and so on); understand the symbology of that system (pick up the key from the classroom bulletin board when leaving for the bathroom); understand the psychology of those who use the system; be able to suggest at least one alternative approach to what is causing stress or conflict; support the alternative(s) presented in ways that indicate the suggestion is made to help all concerned; use language the system uses and likes; avoid putting extra pressure on the system's representatives at least initially or going over their heads; and be positive—no "you are wrong" approach, no know-it-all attitude, and no vulgar language. For more help on conflict resolution and related skills, check the latest edition of *Joining Together: Group Theory and Group Skills* by David and Frank Johnson (2000).

Guide and Follow-Up Questions for Teachers and Students

1. Am I evaluating my own level of stress in teaching and in teaching this idea? (I might frequently find it helpful to talk with another adult before, during, and after teaching how to cope with change and stress.) Am I assessing my students' emotional states, their stress levels, as I teach coping with change and stress and the rest of my curriculum—and sending them to other helping professionals, as appropriate (school psychologists, counselors, social workers, speech clinicians)? In other words, am I becoming a closer student of my students?

2. Are my students, with my help, facing their fears and doing so in a safe and protected manner? For example, do we write

poetry, myself included, to identify felt stress (and maybe share these poems without names attached)? Do we engage in volunteer role-playing that portrays an identified stress or change situation and discuss it, perhaps in terms of conflict resolution skills? Do we write stories that may distance our personal stress from ourselves onto something "out there"—other people or situations? (Robert Lewis Stevenson had the ability to cope with writer's stress by commanding the "brownies" of his mind to furnish him with a story while he slept.)

3. Am I aware of professional resources available to help me teach how to cope with change, learn about change theory, and deal with stress? Some good materials are available from Stenhouse Publishers at www.stenhouse.com. Send for their most recent catalog. A useful professional resource on organizational (e.g., school) change is *Conquering Organizational Change* by Pierre Mourier and Martin Smith (2001). For a free examination copy, go to www.ceppress.com/examcopy.asp.

4. Do I look for possible signals of distress among my students? Some signals are general irritability, signs of depression, impulsive behavior, emotional instability, nervous ticks, tendency to be easily startled by small sounds, pain in the neck or lower back, neurotic behavior, excessive sweating, high-pitched and nervous laughter, pounding of the heart, and inability to concentrate. Do I know something of the lives of my students outside the classroom where these signals may originate?

5. Do I have two components in my stress management system for my students: a generalized stress prevention program and a crisis intervention program? The former includes providing education about stress and teaching students some strategies for dealing with it to help them relax (e.g., teaching students to take their own pulse; teaching them to do simple isometric exercises in the classroom—such as clenching their fists and then opening their hands, extending the fingers as far as possible; or teaching them some cognitive imagery techniques—such as envisioning successful outcomes of a task in advance through "the mind's eye"). The crisis intervention component

includes keeping open contact with parents, helping professionals in the school and school system, and being alert to
related legal implications. Depending on the seriousness and
immediacy of the crisis, it also involves teacher actions to protect the child or to get direct aid for the student. It may involve
confronting the identified student(s) with the facts and
together negotiating an agreement or contract.

6. Am I willing to research models for describing and facilitating
the process of change and adopting the innovations resulting
from change as these occur in an institution or system, such as
a school system, and determining what I might borrow for my
own teaching on coping with change? One model is the
concerns-based adoption model (CBAM) associated with
Gene E. Hall, University of Texas at Austin, and the Research
and Development Center for Teacher Education at the University of Texas at Austin.

TEACHING COMMUNICATION SKILLS—VERBAL

Teachers and students live classroom life immersed in verbal communication. It is their umbilical cord to one another. There is "work talk," where voices range from one-to-one conference whispers to louder voices for presentations, and there is "teacher talk," which includes giving information (lecturing), asking questions, giving directions, responding to student feelings and ideas, and criticizing or justifying teacher authority. There is student fluency, where students can speak to others and to the teacher quickly and accurately with appropriateness and breadth of vocabulary. There is self-talk, or intrapersonal communication, where students talk to themselves to guide their actions as they work independently ("I need to count my required number of paragraphs—1, 2, 3" or "I will check to make sure I put my name on every paper") and when they work by themselves with a computer ("Darn, I need the teacher's help to run this program"). There is "read aloud," discussion, and debate; classroom skits, dramas, role-plays, and productions; and multicultural peer tutoring, all giving students opportunities to use and stretch and improve their verbal abilities.

In our approach to teaching verbal communication skills to students, we first define verbal communication as orally presented vocabulary students use to initiate, maintain, or conclude conversation with themselves or others in their immediate situation (talking to a friend in class) or more global environment (speaking over the phone to a far-away relative). The major ingredients common to verbal communication are a sender, noise or interference, a receiver, a message, a channel through which the communication travels, and a cultural milieu—including the personal emotions of the sender and the receiver—in which the communication operates. Full verbal communication is achieved when the receiver creates in his or her own perceptual field the full meaning of the message as it was initiated and intended by the sender. That includes the content, the connotations, and the context in which the message lives.

Generally, full verbal communication, up to three-fourths say some researchers, gets "muddled up." A number of useful generalizations can be made about the process of verbal communication. First, it is a dynamic process (e.g., one comment usually leads to another). Also, verbal communication is irreversible; once something is said, it cannot be erased or taken back. It occurs often on more than one level; the message "Chien did three drafts of the assignment" might be meant as a statement of fact or as a negative value judgment, for example. Verbal communication is affected by a number of factors including physical setting, expectations, experience, commonality of interest, style and technique, and the level of trust. It is more effective if consistent with nonverbal communication and utilized along with skills of listening and other skills of interacting.

The overriding idea behind teaching verbal communication skills to students is to develop a significant increase in their "knowing" and "doing" competencies related to effective verbal communication. Some of the advantages of teaching verbal communication skills (and not *only* the required standards) include the following:

- Effective and efficient student verbal ability helps teachers assess what students are learning.

- Learned verbal skills can help students contribute to the class and the curriculum.

- Quantity of interaction between students and teacher (e.g., 1,000 or more interactions per day in elementary grades, many of these verbal) tends to be more effective when both parties better understand, and can use, the medium.

- Ability to converse effectively with other students and with the teacher can enhance student motivation to learn.

- Information gained from the process and content of student talk can help teachers learn more about their students as individuals.

- Student communication skills can contribute to better self-understanding (getting verbal feedback from others) and subsequent healthy self-concept as well as improved understanding of others (e.g., through inquiry questions).

- Growth in verbal skills can enable students to develop inter-community relationships (as among different ethnic groups) and make the classroom a more interesting and enjoyable learning community.

When verbal communication skills are intentionally part of the classroom curriculum, and it is rare when they are, they are mostly illustrated through teacher modeling with the hope that students will "catch on." In this positive verbal environment, teachers extend invitations to students: "Let's talk about your project." And they use praise: "You seem to be quite competent with those formulas." They press students for clear statements of theories and support for their hypotheses. They prompt or give hints to help students verbalize difficult concepts. They state where they are in the progress of the lesson: "I see we have 7 minutes left today; let's do a brief closure exercise." From these and similar skills used by adults on a consistent basis in the classroom to initiate, maintain, or conclude conversation, students may learn and try out effective verbal skills on their own. We believe, however, that *direct instruction in verbal skills* makes more of an impact on student learning and is more consistent with INTASC principle 6: *The teacher uses knowledge of effective verbal, nonverbal, and media techniques to foster active inquiry, collaboration, and supportive interaction in the classroom.*

Work Options

Talking Opportunities

Involve students in many and varied talking opportunities, such as participating in a parent conference (monitored), making a presentation or group report to the class, delivering a speech assignment, describing their feelings (about a piece of the lesson or curriculum), or taking an active part in small group work.

One-to-One Skills

Practice with primary verbal interpersonal communication skills in class drills. Teach them so thoroughly that the students can use *all* of them in one-to-one relationships on their own; remember the thought popularized (DiCaprio, 1974) by the work of psychologist Abraham Maslow: "If the only tool you have is a hammer, you tend to see every problem as a nail." Some of these skills include the following:

- Behavior description—a skill for improving communication between two people that involves reporting specific, observable actions (behaviors) of another without making judgments about the other's motives, attitudes, or personality traits. This skill permits the other person to become more aware of his own behavior. Example: "I noticed that you just interrupted me a second time while I was giving out responsibilities in our group."

- Description of feelings—a skill for improving interpersonal communication where a person offers a statement in which she refers to "I," "me," or "my" and describes some kind of feeling by name, action urge, simile, or other figure of speech. The skill permits the user to clearly state her feeling in order to avoid another's misinterpretation of an emotional state. Example: "I feel discouraged when you (teacher) give so much homework."

- Perception check—a skill that allows the other person to know that you are trying to understand his feelings correctly. It is a statement that describes what you perceive to be the other's inner feelings or emotional state. It is usually followed by a question to check if you are correct in your understanding. Example: "I get the impression you are excited about working with me on this project. Am I right?"

- Paraphrasing—a skill for clarifying interpersonal communication through which you show the other person what her idea

28

or suggestion means to you. It consists of making a statement revealing your present understanding of the other person's comment. The statement is then followed by a question through which you test your understanding—and give the other person some clarity on how she is being heard. Example: "If I'm hearing you accurately, you're telling me you don't want me to include today's writing draft in my portfolio. Am I correct?"

Humor in Communication Drills

Bring some humor into drill and practice with verbal communication skills. Humor can engage students in learning the skills; it can provide a light touch to accompany serious interaction; it can relax tension, reduce inhibition, and add to an "up-beat" classroom climate; it can reinforce a point; and it can help students think more or differently about what comes up in the classroom (recall Charlie Chaplin's imitation of Hitler in the classic film *The Great Dictator*). Some of the basic techniques for achieving humor include surprise or shock, exaggeration, incongruity, alliteration, irony, ambiguity, absurdity, playing with words (puns), and satire. Remember that proper work with humor avoids the use of ridicule or mean teasing or sarcasm to hurt another. It avoids cynicism to pump up the self at the expense of others. It is an indication of emotional health and a playful spirit at work, and it is well worth the effort as smiles and laughter are some of the basic responses that as human beings we all have in common. Here is an example:

Student: "Teacher, my partner swallowed our only lab pencil!"
Teacher: "I'll be right there. What are you doing in the meantime?"
Student: "Why, we're using a pen!"

(Maybe a paraphrase by *Teacher* would have been helpful: "You are saying to me that you need something to write with. Am I on target?")

And here's an actual announcement one of us heard at church during the writing of this book: "Our eighth graders will be presenting Shakespeare's *Hamlet* in the church basement on Friday at 7 p.m. The congregation is invited to attend this tragedy." (Maybe some productive oral feedback would be helpful here!)

Helping Trios

Teach students to work in "helping trios" in order to practice verbal skills and improve their verbal communication abilities (see figure 3.1).

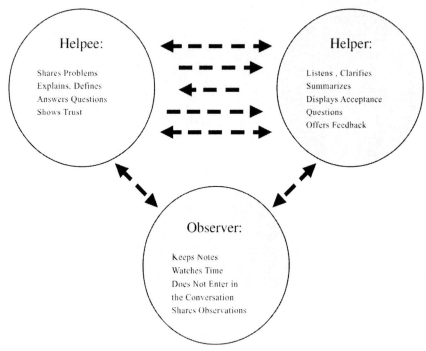

Figure 3.1   The Helping Trio

The Concept of Feedback

Teach students the concept of feedback and have them practice with it under teacher supervision. Feedback refers to the giving and receiving of communication concerning the effects persons have on one another. It includes both intellectual and feeling components and verbal and nonverbal dimensions. Feedback can be a major way for students to learn about their communication abilities. It helps them know whether their behavior is having the effect they want and gives them information for considering changing their behavior. Guidelines for giving feedback include the following: check readiness of the receiver (when possible, feedback should be solicited rather than imposed); be descriptive, not judgmental, and direct the feedback at the performance rather than the person; give the feedback as close to the initiating event as possible and at an acceptable time and in a helpful context; offer a thought or perspective or idea perhaps unfamiliar to the student receiver (something "new"); deal with things about which the receiver can do something; offer specific information; provide a manageable amount; check to see if the feedback is clear to the other person (who may or may not agree with it); and share something of yourself in the process (e.g., some of your own feelings or related experiences or reasons for giving the feedback). Some guidelines for receiving feedback include state what you want feedback to be about; check what you have heard; and share your reactions to the feedback.

Practice Exercises

Invent or locate and carry out practice exercises to help students learn identified communication skills. For instance, with perception checking, ask a volunteer to come up front with his or her back to the class. Ask the class to demonstrate an emotion without naming it, perhaps from a sign you hold up, then ask the volunteer to face the class and work to correctly read the emotion through use of perception checking. (Do not allow "20 questions," but rather insist the volunteer work with the skill. Although perception checking is fundamentally a one-to-one skill, it can be learned through this exercise, and it tends to bring humor into the learning process.) Emotions to use in practice can be identified through a thesaurus, and more skills to work with can be located in books such as *T.E.T.: Teacher Effectiveness Training* by Dr. Thomas Gordon (1974) or more popular self-help books such as *Men Are From Mars, Women Are From Venus* by John Gray (1992) and *The One Minute Manager* by Kenneth Blanchard and Spencer Johnson (1982). Another practice exercise involves students practicing the skills in "live" interactions. Ask students to use any three of the skills four times each before the announced due date. Use may be at home, at school, or in any interactive situation the student desires. This exercise consisting of a dozen attempts or practices uses a three-part format for each use of each skill: the situation described briefly (who, where, when), the actual (as best it can be recalled) quote used by the student practicing the skill, and a description of the results from the use of the skill; even a statement that no results can be noticed is appropriate, if that is the reality.

Guide and Follow-Up Questions for Teachers and Students

1. Do I, as a teacher, check to see how much class time is taken up by me talking and evaluate if this is consistent with student learning? Researchers such as John Goodlad (1986) have found, for instance, that 70% to 80% of classroom time is taken up by teacher talk.

2. Is checking out research on verbal language a habit in the classroom? The more informed you are, such as knowing the human brain appears to be wired to learn language at an early age and that verbal communication is only one small part (about 20%) of total communication, and that of the world's 6,000 or 7,000 languages, a couple go out of business each week (most in the jungle of Papua, New Guinea, or in Indonesia), the more likely you will be able to teach communication skills effectively.

3. Are accommodations made in the classroom for students with verbal expression problems, such as giving them a little extra time to respond or asking specific, structured questions that permit students to utilize the elements of the question to organize their answers?

4. Do you maintain an active search for materials to promote verbal literacy, materials such as *The Read-Aloud Handbook* by Jim Trelease (2001)?

5. Do students in the class actively research verbal language questions that are of interest to them? For example, where did spoken language come from? (One theory is the gesture theory. It suggests that human speech was an outgrowth of what amounts to language pantomime.) After people began to associate certain signs with certain meanings (e.g., a closed fist with "fight"), it could have been a next step to use sounds to accompany the gestures. Gradually the sounds became equal in importance with the gesture and eventually often came to supersede the gesture.)

6. Do you check to see if your verbal communication patterns are different when you, as the teacher, communicate with differ-

ent groups of students—gifted, "slow learners," ESL, boys and girls? Do the differences help or hinder effective communication and learning? Example: Teacher questions encourage intellectually gifted students to interact but do not encourage "slow learners."

IDEA FOUR
TEACHING COMMUNICATION SKILLS—NONVERBAL

Teaching nonverbal communication skills is the counterpart of teaching verbal communication skills. What can be said about verbal skills can be said just as well about nonverbal skills, and their importance in life demands attention in the classroom. Often-cited research by Albert Mehrabian (1968) suggests that communication is 7% content, 38% tone of voice, and 55% body language. Although modern day cell phone and computer "conversations" certainly challenge this breakdown, there are still many nonverbal elements in the many interactions between teachers and students on a daily basis. The reliance on nonverbal communication is not a new reality, but one that evolved from Upright Man as he planned his hunts, collaborated in the killing of prey, and shared the carcasses with his mate and children. Fiorello La Guardia, the flamboyant New York City mayor in the 1930s and early 1940s, understood the importance of nonverbal skills and their cultural roots. He used to campaign in English, Italian, and Yiddish. La Guardia had one set of hand gestures when he spoke Italian, another set for Yiddish, and still a third for English. He knew each language was accompanied by its own set of nonverbal gestures.

The reality of nonverbal communication is that in human evolution, politics, or classroom communication, the nonverbal is usually more significant than the verbal. Although we can manipulate and disguise our verbal messages pretty much at will, our bodies are predisposed to convey only our true meaning, and when verbal and nonverbal messages conflict, the receiver of the message invariably relies on the nonverbal. Take, for instance, the situation where the student speaks to the teacher to request a

34

meeting. The teacher responds by (1) saying, "Sure, let's talk right now" and by (2) looking at his watch while making that statement. In this inter-active situation, the more powerful message is the second one, which is likely to close off at least this chance for the student and teacher to talk by suggesting that the teacher really does not want to talk now; he has a meet-ing or something else to attend to. The nonverbal message in the example contradicts the verbal and may or may not be intended, but it is dominant and it is received in line with one or more of three controlling sets of atti-tudes on the part of the receiver: the degree of liking or disliking felt toward the sender of the message, the degree of submissiveness or dominance felt in the student–teacher relationship, and the amount of reaction—positive, negative, or mixed—that the sender arouses in the receiver of the message. Students, in general, expect to communicate with teachers and to be observed by teachers, and they continually send nonverbal messages. They can project nonverbally, for instance, attentiveness or disapproval or any of a parade of emotions, moods, attitudes, and feelings. With alertness to stu-dent nonverbal communication, teachers can read these messages and per-haps see beneath them while remembering that students' nonverbal communication is always a function of place, age, sex, role, and purpose.

Unfortunately, nonverbal communication taught *to* students currently gets very little emphasis as part of the regular science, social studies, English/language arts, or math curricula today. When it is taught, it is usu-ally mentioned in connection with the behavior of characters in literature or animal behavior in science class. The teaching of nonverbal communica-tion also gets some inclusion in the curriculum when teachers teach stu-dents to deliver speeches or make oral reports. A few teachers, if they don't teach nonverbal communication to students, do at least *monitor* their own students' nonverbal communication through devices such as a teacher's log, which identifies the students' nonverbal communication (room quiet; stu-dents are looking at their worksheets and writing on them), the teacher's interpretation (students are motivated and on task), and the teacher's sub-sequent action (keep the assignment going—this may not last long!). Occa-sionally, a teacher may encourage students to tell stories about violence done to them by using their bodies in dance or pantomime. But, overall, the teaching of nonverbal communication and its skills and understandings is not part of instruction in the standards, and the attention given to non-verbal communication in today's classrooms is insufficient.

Our working definition that teachers can use when teaching nonverbal communication is that nonverbal communication is *language without words*. It consists of observable message patterns of gestures, body style, and movement; paralanguage (e.g., inflection, pitch, pause, rate of speech, loudness, emphasis, adding dialect to conventional words, and utterances without dictionary meaning such as "er" and "ahh"); color, dress, custom; touch; space; travel; time; and smell—all eight of which augment (stomping while shouting), contradict, replace (giving travel directions to the main office to a beginning ESL student), preview (winking before inviting a student to tell *that* joke to the principal), and/or regulate the spoken word ("Tom, I'm pregnant!"). The key to working with nonverbal communication is to recognize that it is absolutely tied to culture. By culture, we mean a set of ideas, beliefs, attitudes, values, behaviors, customs, institutions, notions of history, laws, language, and meaningful symbols that are generally but not absolutely shared by the members of a group at a given period of time. A nonverbal that carries meaning for one person may well not carry that same meaning for another person—even one in the same culture. One American high school teacher reported recently that when she was quietly asked by a student to go to the bathroom but did not hear the question, she looked up and raised her eyebrows inquiringly. Much to her surprise, the student immediately turned and left the classroom. In the Eskimo village where this teacher taught, it is custom to raise the eyebrows rather than nod the head to indicate *yes*. The student had been given permission to do what he wanted to do through a nonverbal sign based on lack of cultural understanding. Both students and teacher need to be aware of the nonverbal dimension of communication and its cultural context, and they need to be competent in understanding the silent languages and their related skills in order to get messages across, reduce distortions, and keep open the interaction and learning in the classroom. In INTASC terms, the teacher *uses knowledge of effective verbal, nonverbal, and media communication techniques to foster active inquiry, collaboration, and supportive interaction in the classroom* (INTASC principle 6).

Work Options

Charting Nonverbal Behavior

Develop a five-column chart of nonverbal behavior resulting from action research by your students and you. Keep it a "living document," subject to addition and change, and consider posting it in the classroom for occasional reference and discussion to improve learning about nonverbal communication. Use the following columns: Nonverbal Behavior Observed; Sender's Cultural Background (as far as can be determined); Probable Meaning of Behavior to Sender; Possible Understanding of Behavior by Receiver(s); Possible Cultural Influence Pertinent to Sender's Nonverbal Behavior. Here are examples of the categories, in order: palm up with fingers closed except the index finger, which is moving in and out; Vietnamese and a recent arrival to the United States; "I am showing contempt and consider you an inferior," or "I am purposely trying to provoke you"; "That person is simply motioning for me to 'come here'"; and this is a typical sign of hostility and disapproval in Vietnamese society.

Learning Centers

Establish learning centers dealing with the eight categories of nonverbal language. For example, one center could deal with Mark Twain's *Huckleberry Finn* (1981), where there is an interesting conversation between Jim, the slave, and Huck, his young friend. Huck has told Jim that the Frenchman says "Polly-voo-franzy?" when he wants to know "Do you speak French?" Jim objects, and the conversation goes on. Learning at the center could deal with the evident paralanguage in this and other verbal interactions in the story.

Considering Culturally Based Nonverbals

Very carefully, invite students to consider and evaluate culturally based nonverbals. Are some better or worse than others? Are some "right" and some "wrong"? Why? (Culture is loaded with personal feeling and emotion, so be sure to proceed carefully with this work option.) Example: The "OK" hand gesture used in many U.S. cultures may not be a good one to use with students from Latin American countries, where it is a most obscene gesture. Some other acknowledging signal might be better. Muslim girls wearing the hijab, or head covering, may be "right" to the girls and "wrong" for the classroom in the mind of their teacher. In our experience recently, a Vietnamese student complained to the principal that he did not like to be touched, even in a friendly way, because that is unusual in his culture. Be careful out there!

Classroom Listing of Nonverbals

Make a list of nonverbals for use among students and between teacher and students in the classroom. Develop it and check it with students and significant adults (e.g., parents). Give each student a copy, and use this as a nonverbal communication device in the classroom—subject to revision, addition, and change. Example: placing finger to lips means silence; handshake means you did a high-quality job; forefinger raised means a temporary halt; sliding palms over each other means we have a good thing coming; hand up, palm out means temporarily stop. The mirror drill can be used for helping students become familiar with the nonverbals on the list. Students stand up and pair off. One student practices a nonverbal called (by number) from the list by the teacher, while the second student observes it and offers modifications and affirmations (e.g., "good job") to make the behavior more effective. (Modifications, corrections, and improvements could be done *nonverbally* by the second person—using himself or herself as a mirror—if the leader or teacher so desires.) Students continue to stand while the teacher asks them to switch roles within the pair. The teacher now calls out another item from the list for practice. This continues, with the back and forth switching of the one who practices and the one who "corrects" in each round, for about 20 minutes. During (or after) the practice, "stop-actions" are initiated by the teacher. These "freeze" the drill and practice while students and teacher analyze the product of the exercise ("Are we learning the nonverbals?") and the process ("Are the corrections being given to assist learning?").

Pair Awareness

Do nonverbal pair awareness exercises. Example (space and touch): Student A gradually moves closer to student B while they work together on a "project." Student A begins to touch student B and continues to move closer to him and to gradually touch him more and more as they talk and work. Debrief after about 2 minutes: What was going on? How did the two students feel? *Note*: Only student A should be told of the sequence in advance. Example (custom and paralanguage): Student B stares directly into the eyes of student A while the two are conversing about an assignment. Student B continues staring while gradually increasing the volume of her voice. Debrief after about 2 minutes: What was going on? How did the two students feel? *Note*: Only student B should be told of the sequence in advance.

Category Exercises

Practice with the categories of nonverbal behavior. Example (body style, movement, facial expression, and gestures): Class members take turns trying to express various emotions with their bodies. The teacher hands a participant a slip of paper with a situation and the name of an emotion on it; the volunteer student acts out the emotion without words, and the rest of the class tries to determine from the nonverbal cues what emotion is being expressed. Examples of situations include *elation* or *anger* when accepting a trophy as the second-place winner, or *fear* when walking to the front of the room when you have just been called upon to give your assigned report for which you are unprepared. Remember to debrief the exercises with the students.

Locating Examples of Nonverbal Behavior

Have students locate articles about and examples of nonverbal behavior and its categories in newspapers, magazines such as *Psychology Today*, and other media. Literature also works: *My Papa's Waltz* by Theodore Roethke (touch), for example. Students can "cut and paste" some of what they find for display in class, with the following information: identification of item and source (e.g., sports page in daily newspaper); classification of nonverbal behavior by dominant category (e.g., body movement of a baseball player); reason(s) or evidence for the classification (e.g., baseball player's trunk is twisted and arms are outstretched in completion of swing); and possible feelings expressed through the nonverbal language (e.g., wide open eyes and smile suggest good feelings about the home run hit).

Guide and Follow-Up Questions for Teachers and Students

1. Do I "relish silence"? Silence is a nonverbal language that allows the "internal voice" to operate. It encourages reflection and provides time for personal thought and formulating responses. It permits listening to surrounding chatter and judgment as to the possible "falseness" of conversation. It can convey the idea that what has just been said is important and

should be considered or reconsidered. It serves as a reward: "I care enough about you to give you an opportunity to offer what you have to say." It may increase the amount or elaboration of participation by others. It may encourage a relaxed atmosphere for collaboration, including giving time for more quiet personality types to contribute. Remember, silence can result from a variety of sources, such as nervousness or comfort with oneself or respect for others. On the menu of nonverbal communication, silence should not be neglected.

2. Have I experimented with a variety of nonverbal classroom arrangements to facilitate learning in classroom groups (see figure 4.1)? (An excellent resource for K–6 teachers is *Classroom Spaces That Work* by Marlynn K. Clayton (2001), available from Northeast Foundation for Children, www.re sponsiveclassroom.org/bookstore/popovers/classroomspaces .html.)

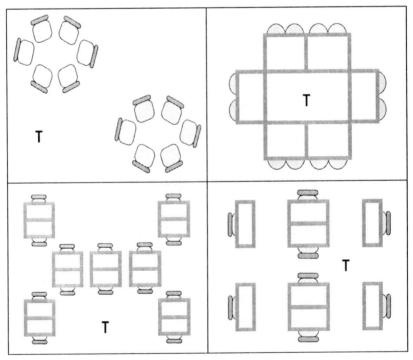

Figure 4.1   **Facilitating Group Discussions**

3. Do I along with the students devise a variety of classroom floor plans to facilitate whole-class learning? (See figure 4.2.)

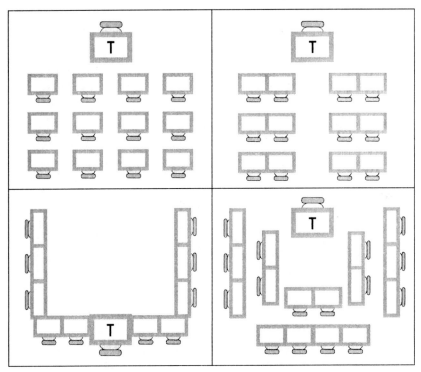

Figure 4.2 Facilitating Whole-Class Learning

4. Do I have a system for objectively recording acts of nonverbal behavior that I can use to provide helpful reports to students, parents, guidance counselors, or other "need-to-know" persons? One such system is that of narrative description in which you describe the larger environment that directly confronts you as observer of the student; focus on the nonverbal behavior of the student but describe (for context) as fully as possible everything done by the student, including all the student's communicative acts; put your own inferences in parentheses; and write your descriptions in simple sentences. Each observation in person or from videotape should take about 12 minutes to be useful. (No problem with supply of nonverbal acts; students are always communicating nonverbally. Even if they "shut

down," they are sending the nonverbal message that "I do not want to communicate.")

5. Am I willing to try some action research projects in the area of nonverbal behavior with interested students (extra credit for them). For instance, does color "speak" through our conscious or unconscious use of it: yellow stimulates creativity; blue encourages meditation and deliberate thought and may dampen level and quality of communication; brown may contribute to students' desire to move around the classroom; red is a most arousing color. How does the density component of the silent language of "space" affect classroom learning? Will an attractive display of books in the classroom counteract a feeling of being crowded (by creating a general sense of well-being)? Will an environment calling for involving activities, such as learning centers, lower any uncomfortable awareness of the physical presence of other people? Could conversations between two students be *dis*couraged by seating the pair alongside one another?

6. Am I analyzing on a continual basis my own nonverbal behavior and my thinking about nonverbal behavior? For instance, do you study your in-class "zone of travel" so that you move as appropriate into the student action areas and do not sit continually behind your own desk? Do you check out your assumptions? For example, one morning your young Vietnamese student enters your classroom. You notice she has long lines of continuous dark bruises on her skin. You are tempted to assume she has been in an accident or is a victim of child abuse, but when you think about nonverbal behavior and its relation to culture, you call her parents and you find her mother has been "rubbing out the wind" to help her get rid of a cold. "Rubbing out the wind" refers to the Vietnamese cultural practice of trying to cure a minor ailment by forcefully rubbing specific areas of the body, and its sign of "success" is the presence of long lines of continuous dark bruises such as those exhibited by your student.

IDEA FIVE
TEACHING LISTENING

Reading, writing, speaking, and listening are the traditional language arts. In the modern age of mass media, effective teachers add "viewing" and teach them in every subject and in every grade. The problem is that "listening" is the language art most required of students (responding accurately to factual questions, participating effectively in small group discussions, following directions), yet it generally gets the least amount of instructional attention and supervised practice time. Along with emphasis on standards, teachers should teach the five overlapping divisions of listening: accurate listening (e.g., getting information correctly), critical listening (e.g., listening for likenesses and differences, distinguishing between fact and opinion), creative listening (e.g., stretching ideas, doing related and individual imaginative thinking on what is being heard, or developing mental imagery while attending to a speaker), appreciative listening/listening for pleasure (e.g., identifying words that evoke emotion and enjoying the style of presentation in musical comedy or the like, listening for sounds of nature), and selective listening (e.g., listening that suits a specific purpose, such as bringing up a specific memory or listening to pick out a main idea). Selective listening may be either good (helps one pick out quickly those ideas that are relevant) or bad (ignoring facts because they challenge one's thinking). Overall, listening can be defined as the verbal (e.g., asking for clarification) or nonverbal (e.g., exhibiting facial expressions) process of reacting to, interpreting, and relating to the spoken language in terms of past experiences and future courses of action. It is both an approach and a set of specific techniques. (It is much more than "hearing.") In the classroom, the ability to listen considerately to a variety of diverse opinions and reflect accurately on what the speakers have said is the foundation of democratic participation; it encourages inclusiveness and respect.

Teachers who do plan to place additional emphasis on teaching listening need to keep in mind the realities of their classroom situations. Students may lack vocabulary or concepts for coping with what is being said; they may lack adequate experience; they may not be "ready" to listen (e.g., unprepared to take notes, not prebriefed on the speaker's style or reliability, or not knowing how to tactfully interrupt the speaker to clarify what is being said). Instruction needs to point out that listening is faster than talking. The average rate of speaking is about 125 to 175 words per minute, but one is able to listen at the rate of 400 to 500 words per minute. It is very possible to take notes, comprehend, observe the speaker, review, and anticipate—all while engaged in the art of listening. In addition, students may have bad habits such as premature dismissal of an idea heard or yielding to distractions while listening or listening in a "hop, skip, and jump" procedure that misses important points.

Probably the most crucial reality is the number and quality of facilitating conditions present in the classroom for teaching and learning listening. Usually, the most recognized of these are positive regard, genuineness, empathy, and trust. All should be in place continuously. Positive regard refers to a caring for another that is not possessive; it is demonstrating "I care enough about you to listen to you," not "I care to listen to you only if you behave thus and so." Genuineness, or "realness," is being who you are without façade or pretense as you listen to another; but it is also not revealing all of yourself as you listen to others and then respond to them. Every emotionally healthy and stable individual should maintain some secrets, something hidden about himself or herself that does not become known to others through the act of listening to and responding to another. Empathy in the listening process involves putting oneself into the perceptual frame of another so as to understand through listening, as best one can without losing one's own identity or objectivity, the other's overt and covert thinking, feeling, and behaving, even to the point of making accurate predictions and providing responses for assisting the other achieve greater self-understanding. The word *empathy* itself derives from the German *einfuhlung* meaning "feeling into," or the kind of response a spectator gives when leaning forward with a jumper in a track meet. Similarly, effective listeners/teachers "feel into" their listening situation. "How would 'I' feel right now if I had the problem this student has?" Empathy is well defined in the classic novel *To Kill a Mockingbird* (Harper Lee, 2002) when lawyer Atticus Finch, trying to help his children understand people's behavior, says: "You never really understand a person until you consider things from his point of view—until you climb into his skin and walk around in it" (p. 24). Trust recognizes that teaching is, at bottom line, a moral enterprise containing constant opportunities to build or violate trust. "Should what 'I' hear be shared? If so, with whom?" "Do 'I' trust that students will listen to and follow correctly the oral directions I give them about the test and thus achieve scores consistent with their abilities?" "Can I trust myself to deal with my own emotional 'blind spots' or intellectual 'red flags' so I can continue to listen—and avoid premature dismissal of what I am hearing?" Along with recognizing and dealing with the realities accompanying the teaching of listening, teachers would do well to place their instruction on listening in the context of the circular process of interpersonal relations described by the Northwest Regional Educational Laboratory (Portland, Oregon) in the 1970s (see figure 5.1).

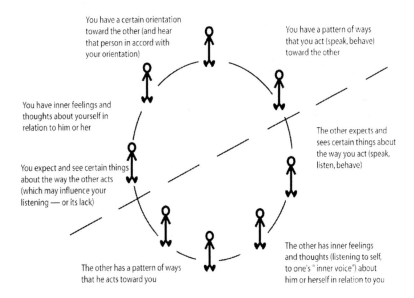

Figure 5.1   Circular Process of Interpersonal Relations

Connected to this process is the actual planned and sequential curriculum for teaching listening, which should begin early and progress throughout a student's educational program in every grade and every subject area. The major goals of the listening curriculum should include helping as many students as possible become active listeners in as many situations as possible (e.g., attending a school assembly, listening to daily announcements, holding interactions with classmates or the teacher, listening to guest speakers, being involved in listening experiences outside of school such as a political rally). A second major goal should be informing students about the importance of listening in every facet of their lives, including school, and helping them learn how listening works in the larger world (e.g., business, marketing). A third major goal is to teach students the skills of listening (e.g., paraphrasing, asking probing questions, seeking central themes) and the steps of listening (e.g., preparing, predicting, connecting to what is known in personal experience, analyzing, reflecting, summarizing). Students need to appreciate that active listening often has many purposes and is usually hard work. In sum, it has been said that a good listener not only is popular everywhere, but after a time he or she knows something. When students listen well to one another, they learn many things and they grow intellectually, socially, and emotionally. Moreover, when teachers teach listening as part of their curriculum or as a special focus, and when they also deliberately and consistently listen to students and act appropriately on the information received, they are aligning themselves with INTASC principle 8: *The teacher understands and uses formal and informal assessment strategies to evaluate and ensure the continuous intellectual, social, and physical development of the learner.*

Work Options

Listening in the Jigsaw

Place students in a jigsaw group (or other cooperative learning group) and let them develop their listening skills in the pursuit of content knowledge. In the jigsaw model, students are assigned to groups of four or five. They read the chapter, handout, anthology piece, or other assignment—in the study of poetry, for example. Then, each member selects a part of the topic for additional study (e.g., the structure of poetry or the language of poetry) and becomes a designated "expert" in this area. The "experts," using guidelines provided by the teacher, meet to research and refine their knowledge with their counterparts from the other groups. They then return to teach their original "home" groups what they have learned. Finally, each original group puts together its information and delivers a report to the whole class at the teacher's discretion. Listening (especially accurate listening) by individuals is clearly necessary in the small group work; it is necessary by the whole class as the final report is presented. In the course of the jigsaw process, which may take several days, the teacher may want to "stop action" to assess with the students the quality of listening taking place and together make any needed modifications in skills and/or process.

Group Roles and Listening

Teach students the different roles people play in groups, and review with them the importance of listening in making these roles work for the benefit of the group. For example, a group summarizer or recorder must listen accurately to pull together related ideas. A clarifier might use creative listening to suggest an analogy or define a blocking term in a new and insightful way to facilitate the group process. An initiator might use critical and/or appreciative listening to offer procedures for dealing with group process ("John is not finished; we need to hear him out and move on ASAP") or for building on previously expressed ideas to solve the group's task. An information giver might make use of selective listening to offer relevant information pertinent to a particular point. A group harmonizer might use his or her overall listening skills in attempt to reconcile identified disagreements and keep all participating ("Mui, we have not yet heard your opinion on this point"). And, a group observer or commentator would use a composite of listening skills to provide information on group growth and expedite the group's evaluation of its own procedures and accomplishments.

Giving Feedback

Help students practice giving feedback. Feedback is based on competent listening and is a way of helping other persons consider changing their behavior because they learn how they are being heard. Feedback is usually offered on a one-to-one basis and provides information about how effective another's work or actions appear to be to the giver of feedback; it helps individuals keep their behavior "on target" and thus better achieve their goals. Students might practice with guidelines such as the following: (1) be descriptive—describing one's own intellectual thoughts, feelings, and reactions—rather than being judgmental (the right to be judgmental must be earned); (2) be balanced—offer one, two, or three points, a manageable amount in total of strong points and points of concern; don't overload—and be specific; (3) be realistic—offer feedback directed at behavior (not the person) about which the receiver can do something, and make the feedback, when feasible, "new" and practical for the receiver; (4) be receptive to requests for feedback—feedback is most useful when it is solicited rather than imposed; (5) be prompt and aware—give the feedback as close as possible to when the work has been completed or the behavior exhibited, and do so at an appropriate time and in an appropriate context (e.g., usually no substantive critical feedback when the student has just a few minutes to eat lunch or is with others); (6) be responsible—check to see if the other person is ready for your feedback and has understood your feedback once offered and what questions, if any, the other person wants to ask now or later.

Remind students that feedback has both verbal and nonverbal dimensions, is given to be helpful, and involves the giver sharing something of himself or herself that is pertinent to the interactive situation. One practice routine is the use of helping trios, in which one student shares a concern, academic or personal, the second trio member practices giving feedback (concentration is on this person's use of feedback guidelines, not on solving the problem), and the third member serves as a recorder. After no more than 3 minutes, the recorder shares his or her notes and all three trio members discuss the work of the person practicing feedback. Roles can be rotated in subsequent practice rounds so that each student gets to practice giving feedback.

Sharpening Listening Skills

Ask students to evaluate a political speech, news broadcast, or other verbal presentation: What is the speaker's purpose? What rhetorical techniques is the speaker using to influence the audience? Is the speaker using fact? Opinion? A mixture? What is important in the presentation? With younger students, try "Bring Me." The teacher tells the students they are to play a game in which they must listen carefully. "Sometimes I will say your name and then say, 'Bring me the chalk or a book, or something else in the room.' But if I just say 'Bring me the window or bring me the wall, you stay quietly in your chair without moving.'" This game teaches accurate listening—for names, for example, as well as critical thinking/listening (some things cannot be brought forward, such as the ceiling or doorway). It also sharpens listening if the teacher lowers his or her voice when giving the directions and if the teacher sometimes uses words that stretch listening and then encourages students to demand and get the meaning of these words.

Listening Posts

Invite students to join in small classroom groups to listen to recordings, tapes, TV programs, and the like. The teacher should have final say in what is selected and should work with students to plan the purpose of the listening (e.g., appreciation of the rhythm of poetry), the time to be allotted, and the evaluation procedure(s) to be used. Having students view videotapes of other students demonstrating good listening habits—and identifying and discussing these—also works, if done with the permission of the taped students.

Measuring Personal Listening

Assign students to survey their personal listening and, perhaps, include the effort as a graded assignment to emphasize the importance of listening. Students could conduct a personal survey of their listening habits, answering guide questions such as: "How much time do I spend each day listening to, say, music CDs?" "Am I at all critical as to what I hear? If so, how?" "Do I really listen in class or give merely 'half an ear' while daydreaming or being distracted in some other way?" "How does my active listening or its lack influence the tasks on which I work?" These surveys, when finished, could be collected and discussed in class without using individual student names. A checklist of desirable active listening behaviors could be developed, and the teacher could do a simple counting analysis ("How many students took notes during the lecture?" "How many demonstrated clearly by their body language that they were most likely listening to the presentation?").

The "I" Message Circle for Building Effective Listening Skills

Teach students the "I" message skill for effective listening, and give them practice in using it. The "I" message, a term used by Dr. Thomas Gordon in his book *Parent Effectiveness Training* (1971), allows a student who is affected by the behavior of another to express the impact it has on him or her and, at the same time, leave the responsibility for modifying the behavior with the person who initiated or demonstrated the behavior. The "I" message helps the other person learn something of the impact of his or her behavior. An "I" message has three parts: the specific behavior, the resulting feeling you received as a result of the behavior, and the tangible effect on you: "When you voluntarily offered your opinion, I felt pleased because it looked to me as if the open communication we are trying to build is working." "When you were talking about your way of solving the problem, I got frustrated because I couldn't do it the same way and I thought I was wrong." Once the skill is explained and demonstrated, gather students in a circle and explain to them that for the next 20 minutes, we (the teacher participates) are going to send "I" messages to each other following the rules on the handout distributed (and reviewed). Only those who wish to send a message need do so; no one should respond to a message sent to them (this is skill practice only); all messages must contain at least the behavior and the feeling; messages must be distributed around the circle—no one person getting too many. When the circle practice is concluded, check with the students if they found the skill valuable. Why? Why not? Will they use it? Why? In what situations? Why not? Should we have future practice circles like this? If so, how should we modify the practice, if at all?

"Listen Up" Activities

Ask yourself, "What examples of ineffective listening have I seen in my classroom?" List ways to create a class climate that promotes active listening (as contrasted with passive, resistant, or some selective listening). Think of students who consistently demonstrate effective listening skills.

In whole-class and small group discussions, identify students who need to practice their listening skills. Set up an extrinsic reward system to motivate the compulsive talkers in the class not to interrupt. Ask students to whisper a phrase or statement to the student next to them. Compare the beginning with the end and go backward to identify the student who heard selectively. Ask students to close their eyes and actively listen to all the sounds they hear in the next 3 minutes. After 3 minutes of listening, the students open their eyes and write a description of all the sounds they heard. Repeat this activity in different environments (auditorium, classroom, library) to sharpen their listening awareness. Play the game "Simon Says" with the elementary students. This works as a check to identify the students who listen to instructions.

Listening for Self-Awareness

Students should try to analyze the words they use to communicate their feelings, state of mind, and opinions. When they learn to listen to themselves, they begin to understand the impact of their words on others. Ask elementary students to analyze and respond in their journals to the following quote attributed to Mark Twain: "If we were supposed to talk more than we listen, we would have two mouths and one ear." Teach students to think "around" the topic and "between the lines." Help them distinguish between hearing and listening. Draw their attention with phrases such as "This is important" and "If you miss this, you will be confused when we move on to the next chapter." Peer evaluation of oral presentations, book talks, and role-playing can lead to the development of critical listening skills.

Reading Connections

After listening to a story the student can answer factual details; summarize the story; and retell the story with descriptive details, dialogue, and characterization. Students can predict topics, guess vocabulary in context, filter out irrelevant details, and learn to use listening strategies for constructive conversations and discussions. In the elementary grades students can listen to directions on a tape and complete a specified task (e.g., draw a flower, write the name of the tallest bird, write a compliment to a peer). Students can listen to a story and create an illustrated picture book for the story. Struggling readers can listen to stories on tape and read along with print versions of the story. Students can take a "listening walk" outdoors and create a story based on the sounds they heard outdoors. Interviewing, maintaining oral journals of monologues and dialogues with peers, and recording communication strategies can help students enhance their listening skills.

Guide and Follow-Up Questions for Teachers and Students

1. Am I genuinely interested at least most of the time in what my students have to say? ("This is a bad time for our conversation to occur. I have a number of things I must do very quickly. Could we meet after school today? If not, I promise to listen to you soon—and always when you really need me to listen.") Do I hear not only students' words but also the feeling tone of what they are saying? Do I evidence readiness to listen, sitting down by my students, for instance, and encouraging them to interact with me and with other students? Do I show respect for my students in the process of listening to them, such as hearing them out and showing enthusiasm for their enthusiasm? In sum, do I set a classroom climate (e.g., avoid a "sit down and shut up" approach) and environment (e.g., avoid room being too hot) for listening while modeling effective listening, and encouraging it ("I am only going to say this once; you will have to listen")?

2. Do I check myself and my students so that we are aware of possible binding responses we may use as we respond to others based on our listening? Some binding responses that inhibit open communication include mind reading ("I know what you mean"); unchecked opinion ("I'm sure we all agree with what you said"); holding to current expectations ("That's exactly what I thought you would come up with"); criticizing on personal grounds ("Why can't you answer like Ben?"); unsolicited advice ("I've had the same problem and I responded like this . . ."); arousing fear/anxiety ("It ought to be perfectly clear to you by now!"); diverting ("So that is causing your problem;

when I was your age . . ."); emotionally obligating ("How could you say that to me when I have done so much to help you?"); denying the other's values ("Oh, that homework isn't as hard as you make it out to be"); ordering ("Don't try it the way you are talking about doing it"); vigorous agreement ("Right, right; that's another great idea"); sympathizing ("Oh, that is too bad; you poor thing"); guilting ("You know if you keep giving me that reason, I'll call your parents and they will really be upset"); discrediting ("Your idea may have worked elsewhere, but it is different here"); put-downs ("From your response, I can tell you are not able to do such a simple thing"); and binding to past behavior ("You are saying that because you always say that").

3. Do I check out resources available for teaching listening, such as the ERIC Clearinghouse on Reading and Communication Skills, National Council of Teachers of English? Another good resource is *Instructor* magazine by Scholastic Inc. (www.scholastic.com/instructor).

4. Do I practice giving empathic responses (and perhaps have my students practice them as well) as we continue to improve on giving feedback based on listening to one another in our classroom? Do we try to tailor responses to a level where the response conveys that the other person is understood at the level at which he is expressing himself (I am aware of what's going on in you, including your underlying feelings—both apparent and subtle—and I let you know). The teacher's responses, especially, might add noticeably to the expressions of the student in such a way as to express feelings deeper than the student knows or was able to express, thus enabling the student to experience and/or come to express feelings in more abstract terms, or helping the student establish why she feels as she does. This higher level response conveys that "I" understand you beyond your level of immediate awareness. And my responses may bring deeper, more significant meaning to our interaction.

5. Do I continue to build on my ability to listen, maintaining a perspective of learning *from* as well as *with* my students? Do I

still enlarge my affective vocabulary of "feeling" words—keeping a thesaurus handy, for instance, so I can respond to students "with feeling"? Do I regularly practice active listening, paraphrasing my students, for example? Do I seek out and experience opportunities in which I can engage in preferred personal listening—musical presentations, school plays, theater (in Shakespeare's day, people spoke of going to the Globe theater to hear a play), oral presentations, and the like? Do I continue to learn and practice listening-building techniques (e.g., using attention-getting phrases such as "I am ready to talk. Are you ready to listen?") and letting students know the purpose for their listening ahead of time so they can better prepare to listen effectively?

6. Do I emphasize that communication is a two-way process? Do I practice active listening and listen without preconceived notions, or do I judge the students based on their accent or dialect? Do I disrupt the student's flow of thoughts by frequently thinking aloud, saying "yes" too often and arriving at a consensus without letting the student fully develop his or her thoughts? Can I identify communication roadblocks and attempt to proactively phase them out?

TEACHING THE EDUCATED IMAGINATION

Asuburban elementary school class and their teacher offered the principal a plan to install by the school playground metal posts that looked like children to encourage passing motorists to slow down. An inner city middle school class under teacher supervision constructed an Imaginarium to create interest in astronomy within science studies. Made from black plastic sheeting held together with duct tape to form a giant plastic bag inflated through a sleeve by a large window fan, students entered the Imaginarium to add their imaginative or real (e.g., the Big Dipper) design for creating a starry, and often pretty accurate, "night sky." A rural high school science class researched under teacher direction how accident, imagination, and serendipity played their parts in significant inventions including penicillin, the World Wide Web, the microwave oven, and Post-it notes. They came to appreciate that chance favors the prepared mind. In these examples, imagination, *educated* imagination, is alive and well and being nourished by teachers as a contributing factor in students' full-blown intellectual growth. It needs to be nourished! All students have imagination; it is part of who we are as humans. Students have active minds that work both within and outside the classroom system ("creative thinker" or "He drives me nuts!") but that are often too little developed or encouraged by teachers fixated on standards. Teachers need to foster educated imaginations to contribute to success with standards as well as with other dimensions of curriculum, classroom, and eventually adult life. Their work on the educated imagination fits with INTASC principle 1: *The teacher understands the central concepts, tools of inquiry, and structures of the discipline(s) he or she teaches and can create*

learning experiences that make these aspects of subject matter meaningful for students.

Teaching the educated imagination in K–12 classrooms mostly takes place through right brain activities that encourage the creative process ("Write your own fantasy") and through teaching students to problem-solve using divergent thinking ("Develop your own graphic organizer from the starting point I give you for this required assignment"). Recent brain research indicates that our brains process information in two different ways. These are connected with the two hemispheres of the brain—the left and the right, both of which work together to help students experience, understand, and interpret their world and how they communicate that understanding and information to others. The right brain's processing tends to be more divergent, visual, symbolic, and simultaneous. It takes care of imagination. It is intuitive. It can create leaps in knowing; it can invent ideas that don't fit into any preexisting scheme or experience—much like the abstract artist or science fiction writer who creates worlds no one has ever seen. Right brain activities such as pretending, mind mapping, and following curiosity ("What is the average life span of a major league baseball?" Answer: seven pitches) build the educated imagination. The main limitation to coming up with activities for building the educated imagination is really the teacher's own imagination.

However they do it, teachers need to keep right brain instruction as a major player in teaching the educated imagination and in helping students learn. Directing learning only to the logical left brain is insufficient. Moreover, teachers who do actively teach the educated imagination do so without making students feel pressured ("You *will* be creative before the bell rings!"). They help students realize that an educated imagination response can vary in length and support—support being, at least initially, perhaps just in one's own mind. A common example, at least in English/language arts teaching is the use of fantasy literature. Fantasy literature provides a different lens on the human condition, one free from purely rational boundaries. It gives students chances to explore momentary worlds in the freedom of their imagination (e.g., personal short poems) and experience magic, even fear, that is at odds with their practical sense and their sense of well-being—all within the psychological safety of knowing these worlds and the magic are not real and the fear is manageable. Yet, fantasy literature is not particularly compatible with just left brain teaching ("Memorize the myth on the handout I give you"). Some frequently used authors of fantasy literature in classrooms include L. Frank Baum, the Brothers Grimm, Lewis Carroll, Roald Dahl, Madeleine L'Engle, Ursula LeGuin, C. S. Lewis, Mark Twain, J. K. Rowling, J. R. R. Tolkien, and T. H. White.

Imagination defined focuses on the power of the mind to create or form an image of something unreal or extend a perception of something already known. It is one of those words that can have a positive or negative connotation. "Don't let your imagination run away with you" is most always seen as a criticism. Unchecked imagination can be deceptive or just simply foolish. While writing this idea, the authors came across a news story from Modesto, California, that reported the arrest of a man for trying to hold up a Bank of America branch. He used a thumb and a finger to simulate a gun, but unfortunately, he failed to keep his hand in his pocket! Imagination can be also destructive to one's own intellectual progress and can lead to mental health conditions such as paranoia. Imagination needs guidance, checks, and balances. Students must be able to discern what is real from what is fantasy; they need to apply analysis and evaluation to stay within legitimate, but not necessarily conventional or constraining, social, moral, and ethical boundaries, hence the *educated* imagination. Perhaps the main check on the educated imagination is a high level of emotional intelligence, which has been defined as intentionally making your emotions work for you to guide your thinking and behavior in ways that enhance your ability to satisfy your needs and obtain your wants.

Daniel Goleman (1995) the guru of emotional intelligence, explains that the five dimensions of emotional intelligence are self-awareness, empathy, social skills, knowing how to handle upsetting feelings or impulses, and motivation in moving toward goals. A strong amount of competence in all five (i.e., high emotional intelligence) serves as a control device on imagination and permits imagination to be increasingly *educated* imagination. The five dimensions can be taught by teachers interested in improving their students' educated imaginations; for instance, introducing the class to peer mediation and conflict resolution techniques works for knowing how to handle upsetting feelings and using social skills effectively, if not for all five dimensions.

In sum, the educated imagination should be taught as a positive contributing force in the lives of students. It enables students to respond to learning in a thought-provoking way, perhaps taking an unusual perspective on the topic of the day. It develops the capacity to sustain intense involvement. It allows students to see a connection between what is being studied and their own lives. It permits giving credence to alternatives to the conventional, and breaking with familiar and accepted distinctions and definitions. It hones the desire and willingness to think beyond rigid patterns, to start over and begin again. It also lets students carry on beyond "obvious" limitations of the given and work at the edge of their competence. And, it permits students to explore worlds of terror and fear within the safety of their own reality. Teaching the educated imagination deserves its rightful place in the school and classroom curriculum.

Work Options

"Seeding" Imagination

Teach a unit on tall tales and/or myths, and interactively play about with students on the nonconventional traits of humor and fantasy contained in these pieces of literature. The reading and discussion may well "seed" the development of students' educated imaginations.

The Fantasy Domain

Have students read and work in the domain of fantasy and science fiction. What science is in *Star Wars*? Are there really flying saucers? What are your thoughts about the concept of living forever (*Tuck Everlasting* by Natalie Babbitt, 2000)? What can you imagine now that has never been? What will daily living, including school, be like in A.D. 2030? Products from student imaginative thinking could plaster the classroom walls and give rise to continued discussion.

Story Time

Share stories from students, yourself, parents, and others about use of the educated imagination. Giant Brands, Inc., offers collections of stories in its free *Profiles in Excellence* pamphlets available in quantity at supermarkets each year. The story of African American inventor Otis Boykin, best known for his creation of the regulating unit for the first heart pacemaker, is one example from the 2003 edition. Another source for stories is popular books such as *Chicken Soup for the Soul*, edited by Jack Canfield and Marck Victor Hansen (1993).

Working With Multiple Intelligences

Offer students a variety of learning experiences on an ongoing basis that activate their multiple intelligences. (See Howard Gardner's and Linda Campbell's writings on multiple intelligence theory in the references.) Especially provide experiences requiring intrapersonal intelligence and visual/spatial intelligence in order to help students build their own educated imaginations. For the former, try having mathematics students track their own thinking patterns for different kinds of math problems; "How do 'I' proceed?" "Do 'I' ever try a new approach?" "What mood changes do 'I' go through as I work math problems?" For visual/spatial intelligence try, in science, something like this: "Pretend you are microscopic and can travel in the bloodstream; draw what you see."

Self-Reinvention

Have your students reinvent themselves. For instance, they might pick a job or career in which they are interested that relates to the subject field(s) you are teaching (math, science, and so on). Then, they should think backward as a person in that career to the present time. "How do I view myself as a student and as a person from the future perspective of the career I am now imagining?" "How does my career feel? What do I like and dislike about it?" "What traits, skills, understandings, and attitudes do I have that carried over from my school days before my present career? How can these be best used?"

Alone Time

Allow students alone time wherein they can learn to be alone but not lonely. A good book, for instance, allows you to be alone but not lonely. So do mental organizing, preparing for the time ahead, practicing metacognition, or thinking about (your) thinking, including whether you have an educated imagination—and at what level it functions. Alone time could be 7 minutes before class ends or during class as a break from the scripted instruction.

Guide and Follow-Up Questions for Teachers and Students

1. Do I watch for extreme adaptations of the educated imagination being played out in a nonhealthy way that could harm the students themselves, other students, or adults? Do I share evidence, even suspicions, of this with the proper authorities?

2. Am I continuing my professional reading on the educated imagination by reading seminal books such as Bruno Bettelheim's *The Uses of Enchantment: The Meaning and Importance of Fairy Tales* (1976) or Daniel Goleman's *Emotional Intelligence* (1995)? Do I make use of commercial materials to help me teach the educated imagination (e.g., Crayola's aids available through www.crayola.com/successguide)?

3. Am I learning to let go and relinquish (some) control over the curriculum to my students, recognizing that such freedom can stimulate students to imagine for themselves what should be in the course, ignite their passion for learning "out of the box," and allow them to predict what they will gain from the course? It also means I have to hold the mind-set that some student ideas might be better than mine or be ones I had not imagined myself.

4. Are the students and I curious, and do we show that curiosity in our daily classroom "doings"? Do we ask questions of one another about things that are unfamiliar? Is there lots of interesting "stuff" around the classroom that provokes student curiosity and makes them eager to "check it out"? Do we engage in activities (e.g., field trips) that cause our mutual curiosity about them and from them to "jump start" our educated imaginations?

TEACHING MANNERS, CHARM, AND SHAME

Shame is dead in American schools and classrooms. Students kiss and grope in open view in high school hallways, plagiarize for assigned reports without remorse, engage in side conversations during school announcement time, and monopolize class and small group discussions. Even teachers (a few) do not invoke a sense of shame in their students, evolving out of a conscience that distinguishes between what is "right" and what is "wrong," and allow students to "put down" other students during instruction time, or put down students themselves: KISS—"Keep it simple, *stupid.*" These are inappropriate and out of line with professional teaching. Rather, a proper sense of shame needs to be in place in the classroom and in individuals in order to put a check on such actions and comments.

Along with manners and charm, shame can be taught, even with serious time spent on teaching to the standards. Teachers in ancient Greece used to beat their students for writing rather than memorizing their lessons. Beating is clearly not consistent with teaching manners, charm, and shame, but memorizing, or other methods, will get the task done—or at least started. And manners, charm, and shame do need to be taught. Certainly, they can be taught as part of a teacher's understanding and using *a variety of instructional strategies to encourage students' development of critical thinking, problem solving, and performance skills* (INTASC principle 4). Manners, charm, and shame were once taught—during the Renaissance. Before that, Europeans spat, belched, blew their noses without inhibition, bawled at each other when aroused, and sulked when their feelings were offended. It was the Italians of the Renaissance who first taught more polite habits. Books of etiquette began to appear, of which the most successful was Castiglione's *The Book of the Courtier* (1976) (the "courtier" was ancestor to the "gentleman"). The ideals of Castiglione's book were inculcated as a code to live by for centuries by private tutors and in the schools. (With teacher help, students today could develop their own code for manners in their classroom.)

Manners, charm, and shame take their most obvious current meanings and have their practice (or lack of it) in the reality of classroom diversity. One example is that of sex-role stereotyping, or the attribution of specific behaviors, abilities, personality characteristics, and interests to one sex. Behavior that results from such stereotyping (e.g., sex-segregated seating in the classroom, unequal assignments for males and females) holds a shameful place in the life of the classroom; it lacks manners and charm, and when it denies opportunities, privileges, or rewards because of sex (sex discrimination), it is in violation of federal law (Title IX). In addition, manners, charm, and shame are further defined in work with ESL students. These students often lack the cultural understanding, background information, and experience for connecting to new learning; they are short on key concepts and vocabulary required for success, especially in science, social studies, and English/language arts. As a result, they may *incorrectly* feel ashamed of themselves (and the teacher needs to point that out) or be treated with a lack of manners and charm by *others* in the classroom. Again, here is a job for the alert, professional teacher in changing student behavior. Shortly before the start of an achievement test administered to a group of Mexican Americans new to formal schooling and American English, some of the students began moving about to ask others for answers. When the frantic teacher yelled that they were wrong to do that and that they were supposed to work individually, one student politely wanted to know "why." "If Sanchez knows the answer, then we all know the answer because Sanchez will tell us," announced this student, with her own kind of cultural logic, charm, but *mis*understanding of standardized testing procedures. Often students hold a very sensible view of life in classrooms. Shame may not always have an appropriate place where it may seem to be needed by less aware teachers. (It's a cultural, cooperative thing with Sanchez and his friends, not an act of which they should be ashamed.)

On the other hand, shame may well be earned or deserved; overall, a legitimate sense of shame should be present and developed and monitored by the teacher in today's classrooms. Multicultural, ethnic, and religious diversity are other areas in which manners, charm, and shame are defined in the classroom either by their use or by their absence. ("You have a religious objection to our class activity today and would like to be excused from participating? I respect that and will give you a super challenging alternative activity. I'd also like very soon to hear more on what your religion has to say about the class activity.") In addition to the teacher's own efforts in manners and charm and to instill in students a proper sense of shame, students need to be exposed to positive images in their own culture or ethnic group with which to identify and relate and thereby not feel unjustified shame (e.g., by being "out of it" or "different"). They also must note that there are often more differences within a group than between two groups in a multicultural classroom (which all classrooms are). These differences, wherever they occur and whoever is involved, need to be treated with the manners and tolerance and respect they deserve. In the view of the American Association of Colleges for Teacher Education (AACTE), multicultural education is education that values cultural pluralism, and to endorse cultural pluralism is to endorse the principle that *there is no one model American.*

One other frontier for the placement of manners, charm, and shame is that of working with learning disability students and "slow learners" in the classroom. Charles Darwin, a lifelong stammerer, was an underachiever in school and was publicly rebuked by the headmaster for his revolt against what he considered useless subjects and for his indifference to the educational process. Schools should be there to help students "Be All That You Can Be," in the motto of the U.S. Army, rather than make students achieve in spite of their formal education. Proper application of manners, charm, and shame can help. (Students like Charles Darwin can be recognized by the teacher and other students through applause and/or polite comments when they raise their scores on tests or assignments or offer a creative idea for contributing to the learning process.) In sum, the teaching of manners, charm, and shame includes teachers teaching themselves to use manners, charm, and shame with students (and evaluating themselves on that use) and teaching students to use these attributes and show them in their behaviors with one another and with their teachers.

Telling a "talk and chalk" teacher she babbles in class, for instance, might more charmingly and politely and productively be replaced by the student inviting the teacher to the student's soccer game and using that venue to lead to future talking about the student's learning style and how the continuing lecture approach being used in class is not really being very beneficial to the student's learning.

Overall, private schools, parochial schools (e.g., Catholic), and some charter schools are the most likely to teach manners, charm, and a sense of shame when they develop and implement a caring classroom environment. Teachers in these or public school settings who use cooperation and collaboration as well as competition to foster academics in a "community of scholars" often teach accompanying social skills that can develop manners, charm, and an appropriate sense of shame. No matter the type of school (private or public) or classroom (authoritarian or cooperative), regardless of the strategies employed (lecture or laboratory), whether with students from different cultural and ethnic backgrounds or so-called "regular" male and female students, teachers should make the time and select materials and methods that are free of racial, sexual, ethnic, linguistic, intellectual, and socioeconomic bias to teach manners, charm, and a legitimate and proper sense of shame in the K–12 classroom.

Work Options

Cotillion Time

Hold a class cotillion. Parents could serve as advisors and be present to assist in its running. The cotillion would perhaps be especially appropriate for upper elementary and middle school students. It would include a full spectrum of manners in all types of social situations. Look in popular etiquette books in libraries for guides.

Learning Through Literature

Use children's and young adult literature to help students read about male and female characters who use manners, charm, and shame in proper context and with appropriate perspective. Give students a chance to discuss why they identify with the character(s), or why they do not. For example, in the story of Cinderella, the wicked stepmother and sisters *should* feel shame. In *Journey to Topaz* by Yoshiko Uchida (2004), Yuki can't understand why she has to live in a concentration camp with her Japanese family. She didn't bomb Pearl Harbor. She's an American and doesn't accept the sense of shame being thrust upon her. Or, try *The Learning Tree* by Gordon Parks (1987); it deals with growing up in the South as seen through the eyes of a young black boy. There is much shame in the society around him to discuss in this book.

Teaching Group Skills

Teach students small group roles and related skills so they can be courteous leaders or followers as their role dictates, and give them supervised chances to fill these various roles in pursuit of academic learning. For example, the "energizer" is a process-oriented group member who is an effective listener and facilitator of involvement, conflict resolution, consensus building, and feedback. He or she is a positive "people person" who is supportive, considerate, enthusiastic, and tactful but who also may see process as an end in itself and may not give enough emphasis to completing group assignments. More identified group roles are found in specialized texts such as *Groups: Theory and Experience* by Rodney Napier and Matti Gershenfeld (1993).

Personal Practice

Ask students to read advice columns in newspapers (e.g., "Dear Abby"); discuss the questions and answers in class in terms of manners, charm, and shame. What honest advice would the students give to the questions posed? Maybe they could organize an advice column within their own class, perhaps as a writing assignment responding to a real question offered from the class but without an identifiable name. Criteria or rubrics for the writing would help objectify students' thinking and perceiving related to development of manners, charm, and an appropriate sense of shame in themselves and others.

Stereotyping and Shame

Talk about sex-role stereotyping in society so that both girls and boys become more aware of it (e.g., the "glass ceiling" situation in some workplaces, where women can rise only to a certain managerial level simply because of their sex). Have both yourself and your students check instructional materials in your class to look for and deal with any sexual or other bias that may be contained in them (e.g., linguistic bias: insurance *man* should be insurance *agent*). Point out connections between stereotyping and prejudice and a sense of shame that should be incumbent upon those who operate through these devices.

Case Studies

Organize students for academic content case studies with partners from cultures different from theirs *or* with partners with similar linguistic backgrounds. In the former, students learn more about the multicultural world in which we all live, and in the latter arrangement, students can help one another understand complicated instructions, which will save time for the teacher. Both arrangements are good for fostering manners and charm in interacting. As a warm-up to case study learning, discussion, debriefing, and its accompanying supervised practice with charm and manners, you could invite a parent to do a guest presentation on manners, charm, and shame in Japanese culture—or whatever, depending on the cultures available to you and the willingness of parents. Remember to ask: "What did all of us learn from this parent's presentation?" One excellent illustrative case study (for American history) is that dealing with Chief Joseph, the Native American general of the Nez Perce tribe, his running battles with U.S. troops over 1,500 tortuous miles of wilderness, and his simple but moving "I will fight no more forever" speech. The Chief Joseph case also offers an historical and intellectually thought-provoking view on shame at a national level.

Guide and Follow-Up Questions for Teachers and Students

1. Am I aware of resources for gaining more information and materials for teaching manners, charm, and shame, resources such as *The Respectful School* (2003) by Stephen L. Wessler with William Preble (shop.ascd.org) or those available from Research Press (www.researchpress.com)?

2. Am I honest with myself in believing that teaching manners, charm, and shame is well worth my planning and instructional time and effort? Am I at least willing to give this teaching a chance, if I have my doubts? Gestalt psychologist Fritz Perls (c. 1969) believed that the average person lives only 5% to 15% of his or her potential at the highest. A person who has even 25% of his or her potential available is already considered a genius. So, according to Perls, (about) 85% of our potential is lost. The authors suggest some of that lost potential could be realized through the teaching and use of manners, charm, and shame.

3. Are my students (and am I) consistently studying, evaluating, and modifying our work with manners, charm, and shame so that they are real in their use, not artificial or phony, and come out of a mind-set that is willing to take risks in the continuing process of understanding and appropriately treating oneself and others? (Videotaping, if available, could work effectively here.) A good example is evaluating our work with preserving the dignity of students with disabilities. Do we generally refer to the person first, not the disability? (Karen, who uses a wheelchair.) Do we employ "normal" etiquette? (People with limited hand use or who wear an artificial limb can usually shake hands.) Do we mention a disability only when it is relevant to a discussion?

4. Do I continue to look for ways to improve the manners, charm, and appropriate sense of shame in my classroom? Do I insist on "please" and "thank you" being used? Do I require students to call me by my title (Mr., Ms., Mrs., Dr.), not my first name, and to identify other students by what they can do, not label them by what they can't do?

IDEA EIGHT
TEACHING SELF-DISCIPLINE

When you are teaching self-discipline in the classroom as a curriculum topic beyond the standards, you are teaching students to regulate or correct themselves for the sake of improvement, certainly including academic improvement. In our working definition, self-discipline is the conscious control by one's own will of the personal desire to speak or act without reflection as to the consequences of those actions on oneself or others. In defining what to emphasize in our teaching of self-discipline, we use the eight skill clusters from the research of Stanley Fagen and Nicholas Long in Maryland and Washington, D.C. As first published in *Instructor* magazine (1976), they are as follows:

- Selection—helping students gain the ability to accurately receive, select, and attend to incoming information

- Storage—helping students gain the ability to retain information received

- Sequencing and ordering—helping students gain the ability to organize actions in a planned way

- Anticipating consequences—helping students gain the ability to relate actions to expected outcomes

- Appreciating feelings—helping students gain the ability to identify and constructively use affective experiences (e.g., "You lost a game. What could someone say to make you feel better and more in control of the situation?")

- Managing frustration—helping students gain the ability to cope with external stress-producing obstacles and interferences (e.g., rain prevents outside recess)

- Inhibition and delay—helping students gain the ability to postpone or restrain personal actions and reactions

- Relaxation—helping students gain the ability to reduce internal tension

Teaching self-discipline is not bonded to isolation from others ("You will be in detention until you can behave!") or to mandates from teachers or significant others ("Do it the way I tell you!") but is ultimately rooted in the relative strength of one's own personality. In the classroom setting, an example occurs when a high school student is encouraged by peer pressure to plagiarize his paper "off the net," and his response is "No, I'll do the assignment using my own thinking." Self-discipline is also evident by students in classrooms when they organize their academic learning time effectively and prioritize their classroom activities, when they take initiative for their own learning, when they follow reasonable directions efficiently, and when they stick to a project and finish it at least up to minimum requirements. It shows when students hold back on quick judgments of others and their work, and it shows through students' willingness to evaluate and modify their own work on a timely basis. These evidences of self-discipline are likely to occur more frequently when the teaching of self-discipline is a planned part of the curriculum.

One primary way self-discipline is taught in the classroom is through teacher modeling. Students who see teachers consistently regulate their own behavior (e.g., responding effectively and efficiently to administrative interruptions while maintaining the flow of the lesson) have opportunities to see the advantages of self-discipline in the workplace and can gain a fuller understanding of what it means to possess self-discipline. Teacher modeling of self-discipline is further demonstrated when teachers consistently manage professionally their variety of classroom tasks, when they promptly fulfill their promises to students, and when they regularly handle classroom behavior problems without losing their own "cool." In a more tangible way than modeling, K–12 teachers who choose to teach self-discipline can do so by refusing to accept work that fails to live up to a student's known ability. It is saying to students that "I have evidence of your ability, and this piece doesn't measure up. I will help you upgrade, but it is ultimately your responsibility. Remember, your reward is (higher grade, self-satisfaction, learning gained), and the consequences of falling short is (lower grade, not being eligible for the team, report to parents)." The idea here is that when confronted with the teacher's "reality therapy," at least some students (not all) will increase their practice of regulating their own behavior for their own continued improvement and decrease their need for teacher intervention.

Another frequent practice for teaching self-discipline is the self-discipline contract, which is prepared by students as an individualized plan detailing what is needed to improve self-discipline and how to go about implementing improvement plans. It includes collaborative effort from parents and teachers. The final and agreed-upon contract may contain clauses that affirm the students as individuals who make their own decisions, who accept the consequences of their own actions, and who do some backward reflection on why their efforts yielded the end results.

Teaching self-discipline in the classroom is also accomplished by providing students time to be introspective, time to reflect on their own degree of self-discipline as it is in the here and now. Some alone time a few minutes before class ends encourages reflection, as does journal writing and possibly sharing, or a combination of the two. Students can reflect on their own self-discipline abilities, or use for comparison or contrast the self-discipline abilities—or lack thereof—of others they know: friends, parents, sports heroes. The introspection is for the student's benefit and personal growth and need *not* be shared. In addition, where self-discipline is taught beyond the standards, it is often done through the teaching of conflict resolution techniques. An example is "peace tables" in the classroom, where students are encouraged to meet peacefully to work out under self-control their own conflicts. A trained (student) mediator can be added to each table to provide structure and underline the importance of the process, which permits all parties to solve the problem to their mutual advantage—a win–win outcome, with learning for all.

Teaching self-discipline in the final analysis is not exclusively for students who are control problems in the classroom, nor is it to be directed mainly to "slow learners" who "could do better if they just concentrated more." Teaching self-discipline is for all students in all grades, and it can always be improved as *the teacher uses an understanding of individual and group motivation and behavior to create a learning environment that encourages positive social interaction, active engagement in learning, and self-motivation* (INTASC principle 5).

Work Options

Observe and Interview

Ask students to find a willing adult currently working in a job of interest to them. Students should follow (shadow) the person of choice and keep notes on examples of self-discipline performed by that person, especially in the line of work. At a convenient time for both student and adult, the student should conduct a sit-down interview to discuss examples of observed self-discipline (e.g., a hospital nurse at the beginning of her shift changes the "Staff This Shift" sign to show her name, the name of the technician, and the name of the assistant on duty). Why were these examples done? Were they done consciously, deliberately? How does their presence, or absence, seem to affect the overall situation? Interesting and useful follow-up discussion in class could be held on what students find out.

Self-Assessment

Have students assess their own degree of self-discipline and how they can strengthen it. Be sure the environment (e.g., classroom) for assessment is not threatening and is supportive (e.g., shared responses should not be used against students). Assessment could include a written response in journals to the following questions: "How hard do I try on assignments in this class?" "If I want to improve my ability to stick to my responsibilities in this class, what one thing should I do first?" "Am I willing to ask for help before, during, and after work that challenges me?" (Self-discipline includes having the psychological strength to request help when needed.) Students could also be invited to complete worksheets on self-discipline-related topics such as discussion habits: "In a discussion, I get angry when, . . ." "I respond by, . . ." "To make the situation better, I could. . . ." Overall, assessment of self-discipline should serve like the red disclosing tablet given by dentists to help patients see where their tooth brushing still needs work; it shows students where their own self-discipline requires additional effort to build and maintain.

Building Classroom Climate for Developing Self-Discipline

With student involvement, determine a set of classroom rules and guidelines and put them in a positive tone (e.g., "Walk in our classroom" rather than "Do not run"); be careful of too many (try three to five). Post these rules where they are easily seen by all. Let these be part of a developing classroom climate that acknowledges student examples of self-discipline (as appropriate, and often by quiet teacher comment to individuals) and that helps students continually build self-discipline: "I expect you to meet the agreed-upon assignment deadline, and I will remind you in various ways"; "What is your understanding of what is expected, and how are you planning to live up to expectations?" Another move for improving classroom climate is to change student membership in assigned groups frequently and to allow students to choose their own new groups, all the time encouraging them to practice their developing self-discipline skills in the selection process and in the various small group encounters they experience. Also, encourage students to accept meaningful classroom jobs, and where self-discipline is lacking when students do these jobs, focus on solutions over consequences.

Using Multimedia

Bring self-discipline multimedia examples into the classroom and discuss these with students. An excellent example is the video *The Diary of Anne Frank* (www.LibraryVideo.com). Excerpts from *The Journals of Lewis and Clark*, edited by Bernard DeVoto (1953), could be put on transparencies and shown on the overhead projector to provide other clear examples of self-discipline that will appeal to most students.

Scenarios for Practice and Analysis

Ask students to produce simple role-plays that demonstrate self-discipline or its lack. Volunteers could play out the roles in front of the class with subsequent class discussion, concentrating on the place of self-discipline as it relates to the scenario. The role-plays could come from the students' own experiences, but need not be identified as such. An example: Carlos is returning to class after a suspension for hitting other students. He is a big fellow with low grades who seems bright enough, but many students are intimidated by him; he approaches Sylvia, a cheer-leader, just before class begins and asks to copy her notes from the last few classes. Show the interaction that follows.

Create and Identify

Create a chain story with students in your curriculum area (math, English, history) about a character who lacks—or demonstrates—significant self-discipline; reflect with students, at several stop-action points, on examples of self-discipline, the outcome of these, the character's likely motivation behind the self-discipline, and ways the character could implement appropriate change based on the self-discipline. (A chain story is one where students take turns picking up the story where it was left by the preceding student.)

Guide and Follow-Up Questions for Teachers and Students

1. How might a student's strong personal self-discipline enhance opportunity for meeting individual goals, such as improved academic achievement? Reflection on this could center on better study habits, more attention paid in class, greater preparation for standards assessment tests—or no noticeable payoff at all. There are no guarantees in teaching self-discipline!

2. Can I as the teacher determine the roots of student self-discipline? For example, one of the authors experienced an incident when some Pakistani girls mysteriously stopped eating lunch. First guess was that the teenagers were on a self-imposed diet, but a call to the parents uncovered that they were fasting for the Muslim holiday of Ramadan. Both adhering to a diet and fasting for a religious holiday can be evidence of self-discipline, but from far different motivations. (In the context of self-discipline, it is usually helpful for the profes-

sional teacher to know what he or she can of why students are directing themselves to do what they do, since most student actions are meaningful at least to *them*.)

3. Where can I as a classroom teacher find out more ways to teach self-discipline? One answer is to keep informed about related high-quality publications such as *Teaching Children to Care: Classroom Management for Ethical and Academic Growth, K–8* by Ruth Sidney Charney (2002). Look in books like this for research-identified teacher skills that will help build self-discipline, skills such as "explains exactly what is expected," "is organized," "ascertains whether students have the same understanding of classroom rules and procedures as does the teacher," "is consistent in communication," "helps students cope with problems," "monitors student work and progress," and "gives feedback."

4. What encompassing instructional and personal approach should I, the teacher, use consistently in the classroom and school environment to nurture self-discipline? (We recommend treating students with civility, dignity, and respect, all within a framework of positive expectations.)

IDEA NINE
TEACHING PERSONAL PHYSICAL FITNESS AND MENTAL HEALTH

We're talking here about lifelong wellness of mind and body. There are no guarantees at any stage of life, but things can be done to facilitate wellness. And, those things start at home and continue in a school and classroom setting where physical fitness and mental health are as important to the curriculum as are academic standards in teaching the whole child to be successful in school and as an adult. A growing body of research in the last 10 years highlights the direct connection between students' health and their academic achievement. If kids are well nourished and active, for instance, they perform better.

The offshoots of physical activity, or its lack, are plentiful. Feeling physically in shape contributes to a sense of well-being, which in turn can increase willingness to take a risk within the academic curriculum and learn, say, a new standard with its attending chance of failure or relearn one already introduced. Success in kinesthetic, or physical, movement activities in the classroom can increase self-reliance, and self-reliance can be extended to everything else in the program of studies. As for the bigger picture, multiple studies show that students who participate in sports are less likely to smoke, consume illegal drugs and alcohol, miss classes, drop out of school, and become pregnant. In addition, for those involved in regular exercise, self-esteem tends to rise, and the ability to solve problems, handle adversity, and be creative improves. We know enough already about the opposite. We're fat. According to the U.S. Center for Disease Control and Prevention (ASCD, 2004), more than 15% of our young people ages 6 to 19 are overweight. And the percentage has more than doubled in the last 25 years. In fact, as a country, we've never been fatter. That is sad news. But what is even sadder is that our children are on pace to be significantly fatter than we are by the time they reach adulthood. With that comes an increase in diabetes and a shorter life expectancy, as well as other scary health implications.

No longer can teachers count on physical education classes to help students choose physical fitness over physical fatness. Required daily physical education for students K–12 is steadily declining (when budgets are tight, physical education is easy to chop); by high school, most students are basically finished with physical education. Even recess time is being cut back in favor of academics. The job of teaching students personal physical fitness, like so many others, is left rather strongly to classroom teachers who are willing to teach physical fitness and mental health along with attending to the standards. How do they do it? One answer is by collaborating with the physical education teacher and coming up with exercises that can be done in a few minutes of classroom time to provide a break from academic class business and to help students get back to the job of learning refreshed. An example is the seated shoulder press. Students sit with their backs straight against the backs of their chairs. They place their feet flat on the floor and tighten their abdominal muscles. Using one lightweight book in each hand, they raise their hands to shoulder level, keeping their elbows bent and out to the sides. They slowly raise their arms over their heads and lower to the starting position. The students complete up to three sets of 12 to 20 repetitions.

Classroom physical exercises may also be connected to the standards. For example, some teachers have students practice their measurement skills in mathematics by measuring the distance covered when they jump, leap, or hop around a designated space in the classroom. One teacher we've heard about, as part of a science respiratory unit, has students create a three-column chart with the headings *date*, *pulse at rest*, and *pulse after activity*. Then, he has each student record his or her pulse at rest. Next, students do a vigorous activity such as jumping jacks. Students record their pulse again after about 3 minutes of the activity. At the end of 2 weeks, students use their data to find mean, median, mode, and range of resting versus active pulse. Finally, they use the statistics to build double-line graphs with both pulses and write a paragraph comparing and contrasting the graphs and stating what they learned.

To teach physical fitness, teachers must provide such exercises on a regular basis. They need to help students develop a positive attitude about exercise and a habit for doing challenging exercises they feel willing and able to do. Moreover, students need to be encouraged to develop a continuing personal physical fitness program both in school and class and outside of the immediate educational environment. (This could include participation in team sports, individual competition such as father–son tennis, or individualized personal programs for physical fitness.) For comprehensive assistance in helping students develop personal fitness, we recommend the President's Council on Physical Fitness and Sports at www.fitness.gov. The council's goal is to make physical fitness a natural part of our daily lives, to provide alternatives for the 65% of American adults who live sedentary lives, and to help kids get presidential recognition (a patch) for fitness, if they want it (www.presidentschallenge.org).

INTASC principle 10 picks up on the importance of teaching personal physical fitness and mental health with its statement that the effective teacher *fosters relationships with school colleagues, parents, and agencies in the larger community to support students' learning and well-being.* Student well-being cannot be defined without a mental health component. Scientists today are finding more and more that the mind is intimately intertwined with the body. Disorders of the brain, for instance, can send out biochemical shock waves that disturb the rest of the body and potentially make learning and an optimistic outlook on academic life more difficult. An unhealthy body (lack of exercise) can lead to debilitating feelings of excessive stress, which hinder good mental health. Pills alone are not the ideal answer to mental health problems such as some forms of depression. Even problems of the brain (e.g., attention-deficit/hyperactivity disorder) are often overdiagnosed or too hastily prescribed, with the result contributing to poor mental health through responses to incorrectly assigned labels, for example.

In one way of thinking and acting that contributes to sound mental health, students could be invited into talk therapy (one to one and not mostly by e-mail) and receive counseling from teachers, including referrals to mental health professionals. Another technique that some teachers use to bring about desirable mental health (through positively affecting the brain's wave patterns) is the employment of music in the classroom setting. They use music to match the mood they wish to create; a business-like mood for the start of class, for instance, could be created by consistently playing a particular cuing song or by turning down the volume of background music playing as students enter the room. Still another technique is the advance organizer strategy. An advance organizer (sometimes called an open loop) is anything that stimulates the natural focusing mechanism of the healthy brain; it could be a teacher's provocative statement, a particular action, or a classroom visual device to arouse learner curiosity on a conscious or unconscious level for what is about to happen. Attention to the focusing mechanism of the brain enables teachers to deliberately direct student attention to the most important aspects of intended learning and can positively affect long-term retention.

However they choose to teach mental health, teachers benefit from having a cognitive picture that defines the mentally healthy student. Remember as you read the following description that one can be mentally healthy without presenting all of the characteristics mentioned. And, teachers will not have "failed" if young people leaving their grade levels do not show all of these characteristics or do not show them in abundance. Teaching mental health, after all, is a way to facilitate student travel toward an academic destination and toward being a mature and caring adult. First of all, mentally healthy students are continually growing. They look forward to discovering, modifying, and redefining themselves as potentially better persons. Moreover, they are basically happy with themselves and where they "are" and hold a sense of personal adequacy, although further growth might involve becoming what even they did not know they could be. Mentally healthy students are real, authentic, and very human. They know themselves and accept their own social, psychological, and physical needs (e.g., exercise). In addition, they acknowledge and deal effectively with the gamut of their own feelings—grief, depression, boredom, anger, curiosity, joy. They can communicate these needs and feelings unambiguously. They can react with resilience to feelings such as those of disappointment, contradiction, or distress. In addition, they trust their feelings and intuition and maintain an inner balance between these and analytical reason.

Mentally healthy students are not distorted in their lives by unrealistic desires, fears, hopes, rumors, false optimism, or pessimism. They are honest and open with themselves as well as with others. They know, for example, that they make mistakes. But they also know that new learning can result, new perspectives can be gained, and problems can be solved with the help of studied past experience, which includes looking at errors as well as successes. In their personal valuing of others, they esteem authenticity and integrity and reject phoniness and sham. Their values for themselves and others are carried out through their daily behavior. They refuse to live totally, for example, behind any role or label—such as "jock" or "slow learner." They are open to life and the experiences it offers; they can trust others but are not naïve or unable to analyze situations and people for what they truly are and have to offer. They have moments of peak experiences (such as setting the school cross-country record) when they feel at one with self and their world, moments when the process of growth has momentarily ceased. Mentally healthy students lack arrogance and readily seek out, evaluate, and accept, when appropriate, constructive criticism. They hold strong convictions yet inspire trust from others. They are goal oriented, choosing and pursuing realistic goals that are important for themselves. They are self-motivated and self-disciplined, especially for activities in which they choose to engage. They are self-controlled yet flexible and spontaneous. They show courage and take risks. They demonstrate a continuing spontaneity and freshness of appreciation; pleasures, for them, do not necessarily diminish with repetition. They can enjoy nonsense, fantasy, and laughter while maintaining a nonhostile sense of humor.

Mentally healthy students have deep and fundamental feelings of identification, empathy, and respect for others as unique individuals having fundamental rights, dignity as human beings, and self-worth, and they communicate these feelings. Their help is actively and freely given because they view their own development as being interdependent with the development of others. It is their belief that behaving in ways constructive to others and the world in which they live (classroom, school) is a necessary precondition for good mental health. They not only are aware of but also search for interconnections between self and their world(s). Beyond holding this action-oriented "external" view, they are also compassionate and sensitive to the needs of others and have the ability to understand others through the "inside," as it were. With this empathic perspective, they can accept errors with reasonable patience and without being excessively judgmental. As a consequence, mentally healthy persons generally have successful human relationships. Their clear perceptions and their sense of self-sufficiency, however, may not make them highly social persons in the "party favorite" sense. Their close friendships may be limited, but they are strongly bound.

On the other hand, mentally healthy persons are not without a capacity for outrage. They see outrage, even violence, as probably inevitable and sometimes justified. (An example from religious history is Jesus' chasing of the money lenders from the holy temple.) They are also constructive in their responsiveness to others. With effectiveness and even joy, they can engage in cooperative relationships in the pursuit of a goal they believe is valid and meaningful. In groups, they can communicate, share ideas and feelings, and function effectively in a nonexploitive manner. They can take into account other peoples' data and ideas and apply logic for verification before accepting assertions. They can integrate their thought to the group rather than always getting their ideas from the group or doing just what others expect of them. They use problem-solving skills and processes to reach fair judgments about group problems and their causes. Basically, mentally healthy students act with and for and through others in their efforts to be useful, contributing members of their society. They seek to achieve what is good for all with whom they are involved, not just materialistically pleasing for a select minority or majority. Mentally healthy students have a strong and positive self-concept. It is based on an accurate self-appraisal and understanding. They like and trust themselves and feel generally competent and adequate while knowing and accepting their limitations. They respect and enjoy their bodies and value strength, health, and fitness. Overall, they have a psychological maturity that enables them to know who and what they are and allows them to define what they believe in.

Realistically proud and independent, mentally healthy students pursue their goals relatively detached from pressures that would have them act otherwise. They gain most of their personal satisfaction from self-evaluation. They show balance in their lives between working actively with others and spending time alone. They do not make undue demands on others, but they do accept advice, reasonably willingly, especially in areas where they are less competent. They have learned how to learn and have found this has given them a sense of freedom. With their personal learning from scholarship and research, for instance, they find they can act intelligently and significantly on concerns when, in their thinking, the appropriate time and place occur. Such "freedom" for them is inexorably bound up with intentional, self-directed, responsible, goal-oriented behavior. Mentally healthy students tend to have a spirituality about them. They believe in something beyond themselves and have a true humility because of it. They contemplate their own existence and the existence of others. This earthly tenure, they hope and plan, will mean something to both.

Finally, mentally healthy students tend to be creative initiators. They prefer an active struggle with life's opportunities and problems. They can assume responsibility and lead or follow equally well. Although they can perceive the deficiencies of certain aspects of their societies, they do not consistently rebel against authority. Although they are deeply concerned with "doing" in a moral and ethical way, they subject their own morals and ethics to inquiry and searching. Essentially, over time, they work out their own values that exercise control over their present lives and guide them to the joy and satisfaction they find therein. They exult not in nonconformity for its own sake but in their personal creative efforts to resolve problems and bring order out of confusion. In their artisan-like approach to performing the tasks at hand, they are self-disciplined, dependable in behavior, and able to evaluate—and accept—the likely consequences of their actions and beliefs. They find additional enjoyment in reaching out for challenge and new experiences, but they can tolerate uncertainty and change in their environment. Often, they take conscious risks to bring about change. They enjoy an optimistic, energetic, vital can-do approach to life and its crises and events. Like Albert Schweitzer comments in his autobiography (1990), they say, "However great the world's evil, I never allow myself to get lost in brooding over it. I always hold firmly to the belief that each of us can do a little to bring some portion of it to an end" (p. 242–243).

To sum up this idea, achievement in school depends in large part on students who pursue a lifestyle of good physical and mental health; healthy students make better learners. Students who are in poor physical condition or who have poor mental health are unlikely to learn as well as they are capable of learning. There are, however, educational approaches that teachers can use to positively affect health-related behaviors among young people. They include focusing on helping students gain skills such as communication and decision making to deal effectively with health-risk situations, addressing social and media influences on students, providing healthy alternatives to high-risk behaviors, using interactive instructional approaches that engage students on an accepting and equal basis, strengthening individual and group norms that support healthy behavior, and providing teacher and other professional support. These can all be implemented by teachers who avoid the tunnel vision of teaching only to the standards and instead include in their instruction attention to developing physically and mentally healthy young people for now and the future.

Work Options

Readings for Fitness

Include the reading of sports books and articles in your curriculum. Consider giving homework assignments on this material and possibly extra credit for things such as finding related "worthy thoughts" such as hockey great Wayne Gretzky's comment in an interview about his Fantasy Camp that "You miss 100% of the shots you never take." (Not a bad thought for developing sound mental health.) Examples of books that are especially good reads are *Seabiscuit* by Laura Hillenbrand (2002) and *Roberto Clemente* by Maritza Romero (1997), a biography in the Baseball Hall of Famers series. An excellent source of articles is *Sports Illustrated.*

Junk Education

Educate children about the dangers of junk food. Work with the school leadership to remove soda machines from school property and replace them with bottled water, fruit juices, protein drinks, or some other and better substitute.

Analyzing the Media

Teach students the techniques used by advertisers, such as paid endorsements from movie stars or athletic heroes, so they are better able to critically analyze the negative nutrition messages bombarding them through the mass media. (It's estimated that kids watch 10,000 commercials for junk food a year.)

Programming Personal Fitness

Require each student to construct, with appropriate help, a personal fitness program and a schedule for carrying it out. It should include plans for both in-school and out-of-school commitment to physical fitness, and it should contain a procedure for keeping track of and measuring results. This program should be signed off on by the student and as many of the following as possible: the student's parents, the physical education instructor, the student's team or individual coach (if he or she has one), and you, the student's teacher.

Meditation Techniques

Teach students some basic meditation techniques (mind relaxation exercises, visualization, guided imagery, centering activities), and have the students practice them in the classroom under supervision. There are many approaches to meditation, some not compatible with K–12 instruction, but its most simple qualities of cultivating silence; encouraging reflection; and allowing the mind to "open," refresh itself, and consciously direct its attention toward something you want to concentrate on can be useful even to the point of decreasing anxiety, providing more tolerance for frustration, and adding to improved mental health.

(An old but good resource on meditation in the classroom is *The Centering Book: Awareness Activities for Children, Parents, and Teachers* by Gay Hendricks and Russel Wills [1975].)

Home Exercises

Help parents come up with simple physical exercises students can do at home without special equipment, just creativeness and supervision. An example is "scrambled eggs" in which two young people or a parent and child walk toward each other from opposite ends of a thin line provided naturally in the pavement or by chalk. When they meet, they work to pass each other and head toward the opposite end without leaving the line. If either falls off the line, it is "scrambled eggs" and time to start over. Another is "stump jump," where a child jumps off a low tree stump and his or her distance is measured. If more than one child is involved, winners can be determined by categories: First place in the (age of the child) group is _____!

Guide and Follow-Up Questions for
Teachers and Students

1. Do the students and I discuss the benefits and downside of competition along with the pros and cons of cooperative efforts and independent actions? These three are all ways of attaining physical fitness. For example, competition can stimulate or discourage and intimidate. Cooperation can give students a sense of belonging or bring about "people problems." Independent action can provide its own individual reward structure or reinforce bad habits such as procrastination.

2. Am I continually looking for, and open to, equitable partnerships between my students and public health organizations? An excellent source for examples of partnerships is *Education and Public Health* by Jenny Smith (2003). It's also a good idea to encourage mature students to volunteer to help out with Special Olympics programs (or even to teach elective activity and health classes at nearby middle or elementary schools).

3. Am I tuned in to resources for teaching personal physical fitness and mental health? Visit www.scholastic.com/instructor for a full and rich array of children's books on health, nutrition, and exercise. Another excellent resource is Stenhouse Publishers. Send for their catalog at www.stenhouse.com. You might want to purchase a classroom copy of a user-friendly book such as *Guide to Self-Care: Answers for Everyday Health Problems* (1999), revised by Philip Hagen and published by the Health Information Division of the Mayo Clinic.

   To learn more about a tool that will help schools measure, document, and demonstrate the effect of student health on learning so schools and teachers can focus on health issues that are barriers to student success, look at ASCD's "Healthy Schools Report Card" at health in education.ascd.org.

4. Do I help students fairly but critically evaluate popular self-help books on physical fitness and mental health that populate the marketplace: formula diet and exercise books, simple keys to happiness books, self-taught positive psychology books and the like? (These may contain some good ideas but also have serious flaws.)

5. Will I consider working to establish a school health team made up of teachers, administrators, parents, and students? Such a team will look at needs in health instruction and physical education and also examine the school environment, health services, and parent and community involvement in school health and wellness issues. The team will serve mainly in a consultant role (trying to avoid starting turf wars) but be assertive in making suggestions and offering creative ideas to authorities and offering help when possible (e.g., recommend to the principal that walking groups around school grounds be established to combat obesity and volunteer to lead them—using pedometers, perhaps). A suggestion for the team to offer teachers is to integrate mental health and fitness themes into their science, math, social studies, and English/language arts curricula. In math class, for example, a focus on nutrition provides opportunities to analyze food by percentage of protein, fats, and other nutrients listed on government-mandated food labels. A physics class could look at how badminton (or other individual sports) incorporates the physics of motion and body movement and promotes kinetic wellness.

TEACHING THE ACT OF ENJOYING

Young children don't much think about it. Adolescents generally deny it (they believe themselves immortal). Teachers often worry about it—but don't especially teach it. *Life is short!* For white men, the average life span is about 73 years; white women's average life span is 79; non-Caucasian males may, on average, reach 67 and females, 75. The point of teaching this idea that goes beyond the standards is to help K–12 students learn to "smell the roses," to enjoy a full life, starting with classroom life, when and where and however they can. There is no shortage of competition for teaching the act of enjoying. On a daily basis, students are confronted with realities that work against enjoyment: neglect from teachers, in-school shootings, classroom bullying, a favorite teacher's suicide, individual pressure to do well on standardized tests, and abuse—physical, sexual, and emotional. The thrill of following innate curiosity that leads to genuine learning and enjoying gets squelched by the pressure for survival.

One thing teachers and schools do tend to do today, unfortunately rather well, is *decrease* the act of enjoying. Elementary school students enjoy school on the whole, contrary to what they might say. Middle school students enjoy at least the social aspects of school. Secondary students, if the national dropout rate is a clue, show even less enjoyment of the academic aspects of education or even of school itself. (Recent government statistics show that the number of high school diplomas awarded across the United States represents only about two-thirds of the 9th graders who entered public schools four years earlier. In *The Condition of Education 2002*, the National Center for Education Statistics reports that over the past two decades, 12th graders have shown a declining interest in school.) Perhaps teaching the act of enjoying can make a positive difference in students' remaining in school and actually liking it. The definitive view we have about *increasing* enjoyment in school is that, when taught, it takes a stand between the real chaos students all too often encounter in their lives and the stifling order imposed on learning by inflexible teachers and overemphasized high-stakes tests. For a dictionary definition of *enjoying*, we favor that of the *Oxford English Dictionary* (2nd ed.), Volume V, which shows the meanings "to be happy," "to exult, rejoice," "to experience pleasure," but also references "to give joy or pleasure *to*," "to *make* happy," thus suggesting teaching the act of enjoying can build individual happiness as well as allow that happiness, or personal rejoicing, to affect others positively in the classroom.

In our own off-beat way of thinking (which we enjoy) about teaching the act of enjoying, we recommend the following four overall approaches:

1. *Teach students to beg.* We're not talking about begging for money as children do in the play *Oliver*, but rather going for knowledge that is new, at least to them, knowledge both within and beyond the regular curriculum. Students need to become increasingly comfortable with multiple sources of knowledge, such as websites and other students (cooperative learning groups). W. Edwards Deming, who is widely credited with laying the groundwork for Japan's major economic boom following World War II, believed that schools should foster students' innate desire to learn (Smith, 2003).

2. *Teach students to be silent.* We believe all teachers should let students have some alone time to sit silently and think and reflect. Often, academic learning that lasts happens not in the activity connected to it, but within the reflection on that activity. During alone time built into lessons, students can silently reflect on what, how, and why they are learning. Moving too quickly from one thought or action to another may create problems rather than embed knowledge. The process of reflection can bring about enjoyment, as can the results.

3. *Teach students to suffer.* Often a little suffering is good for us. True learning, after all, usually begins with puzzlement. Girls can be a puzzle and a cause of suffering to boys in middle

school when girls have already discovered them, but also a way of gaining skill in conducting positive male–female relationships that can serve appropriately for a lifetime. Innate talent is an issue here; the more the talent, the less may be the suffering—in algebra, for example. But so is determination. Repeating science experiments may not be for some students to enjoy, but it can be every student's road to success. A primary job of teaching is to shape the learning environment so that suffering (within limits) is acceptable for students, and enjoyment with or through or without that suffering is available for all.

4. *Teach students to fight.* Students must learn to fight against the bombardment from their culture to smoke cigarettes, illegally use alcohol or drugs, have premarital sex, and do exactly what their peers do. Students need to learn to fight the lure of video games that keep them consistently in solitude and away from interacting with people, ideas, and opportunities. Loneliness is a powerful and potentially destructive force that students need to fight. (One can be alone but not lonely!) Students need to fight to free their minds from settling for only memory learning, which tends to be the lynchpin of the academic standards. Teaching students to fight means helping them gain the primary weapons of higher order and analytical thinking, interpersonal skills, and healthy self-concept. Of course, when this is done, teaching reinforces the subversive component that accompanies good instruction (fighters don't always settle for what authority dictates). "Fighting" also facilitates enjoying the *process* of learning; the joy is in the journey—even with the fights encountered along the way.

Few teachers today teach the act of enjoying directly. Teachers who do attend to the act of enjoying do so *indirectly* by providing personalized learning (e.g., learning contracts, independent projects) and by using flexible grouping that matches students to skills by virtue of readiness rather than the assumption that all need the same task at the same level. Movement among groups is common based on growth on a given skill, and students not only substitute enthusiasm for boredom and lethargy but also can "buy" time for personal enjoyment activities through quick and accurate mastery (100% is not required) of the required learnings. Teachers, in addition, pose to the class high-level questions or problems that do not have easy answers or solutions. "Can you build a Rube Goldberg apparatus that illustrates the science principle we are studying?" As students engage with their individual challenges and group questions and problems, and as their views are thoughtfully considered by teachers on a time-friendly basis ("wait time"), students will find they are enjoying more of the material under study as well as understanding it better.

The dominant way of thinking of teachers who foster enjoyment, at least as a by-product of instruction, is probably "constructivism"—the theory of learning that emphasizes the central role that students' ever-transforming mental schemes play in their cognitive growth. The basic assumption is that people create knowledge from the interaction between their existing knowledge or beliefs and the new ideas or situations they encounter. Constructivism generally casts learners in an active, hands-on role, even to the point of driving some lessons. Moreover, knowledge and understanding are considered highly social; students co-construct them in dialogue with others but ultimately create or recreate meaningful knowledge on an individual basis for themselves. Hands-on activity, working in groups with others, having your ideas and initiatives valued in the classroom, earning and accepting and fulfilling classroom and instructional responsibilities, and gaining learning new to oneself can all be fundamental to fun, to personal enjoyment of intellectual rigor in the classroom.

Teaching the act of enjoying is clearly one idea for which teachers need to save instructional time beyond that allotted for teaching the standards. In sum, teaching the act of enjoying can go along with creating a classroom community of learners and helping all students gain satisfaction from an academic job well done; it is part of what INTASC principle 5 calls for in stating that *the teacher uses an understanding of individual and group motivation and behavior to create a learning environment that encourages positive social interaction, active engagement in learning, and self motivation.*

Work Options

Mentoring

Set up mentoring programs wherein some of your more optimistic students work with your "doom and gloom" and/or isolated students on study skills, test preparation, and academic projects; one or two mentors to about seven or fewer students serves as a guide. The act of mentoring in academics may carry over to mentoring for helping the pessimists and isolates learn a more positive way of living and interacting in the classroom with a corresponding sense of enjoying the goings-on of classroom life. Be sure to be specific about the goals of the collaboration, and monitor the progress of the mentorship. Initiate the mentoring program with careful selection and preparation of mentors, and provide ongoing support.

Field Trips

Arrange, as finances permit, for field trips connected to what you teach. When these are well set up with prior preparation, interesting jobs for the students to do (such as taking on-site notes for questions they have identified), and follow-up back in the classroom, they can be a primary and fun source for enhancing student enjoyment. With focused field trips you can deliberately and/or indirectly teach the act of enjoying.

Taking Risks for Enjoying

Encourage students to take a risk, such as running for class or school office or pursuing an emerging hobby within the confines of school or class responsibilities, priorities, and requirements. Enjoyment is likely to follow risk taking, but so is disappointment and frustration. Part of the job of teaching the act of enjoying is to help *all* these get their just due. (When it comes to finding hobbies to enjoy while in school and after graduation, we are reminded of American humorist Will Rogers's comment that "half our life is spent trying to find something to do with the time we have rushed through trying to save" [*Oxford Dictionary of Quotations*, 1999, p. 632].)

Direct Teaching of Enjoyment

Teach enjoyment directly. "Today we're going to start some activities that will teach you how to better enjoy your life here in school and outside of school as well. The first will be to select a book from the school library that you'd like to read."

Tidbits

Invite students to locate interesting tidbits of *truth* related to the curriculum (or even outside of it). These should be tidbits they genuinely enjoy as they think about their class work. *The youngest pope was 11 years old.* Give students opportunities to share the item(s) and why they enjoyed it enough for sharing ("It's intriguing and it relates to this week's world history lesson"). *The first novel ever written on a typewriter was Tom Sawyer* ("It relates to our readings in English literature, and I always liked Mark Twain's novels"). *It is impossible to lick your elbow* ("That's cool!").

Connections

Have students produce a family history with the help of parents and relatives. It could include family trees, maps showing the odyssey of the family, family anecdotes, "characters," ethnic foods, memorabilia and correspondence from informants, as well as first-person accounts. Ask students to complete a questionnaire indicating whether they are getting enjoyment from the project; if so, why—or why not (and make adjustments accordingly). What is in your family and yourself that contributes to your potential for enjoying life and school (e.g., a sense of humor)? Celebrate androgyny—the concept that people are individual blends of capabilities considered both masculine and feminine according to the traditional stereotypes.

Compacting

Install a process that allows students individually or in small groups to assess to your satisfaction what they know about materials to be studied and what they still need to master. Have them turn in plans with timelines for learning what is not known (and be excused from work on what they know). Offer them the freed-up time to study what they might enjoy studying.

Enjoyment Centers

Construct a few learning stations in the classroom that provide enrichment in breadth and/or depth for students who typically can demonstrate mastery with required subject area work. Allow sufficient time for students to work at the centers, and consider including topics not in the regular curriculum. Monitor in some way(s) what students do and learn at the centers as well as whether they do or don't enjoy what is available there, and to what extent. Change centers as appropriate by using student help and creativity. An example of a center is "Homograph Home." Here students are challenged to rephrase sentences by filling in the blanks with homographs (words that are spelled alike but sound differently). Sample: "She moaned and *sulked* when her *motorized bicycle* was stolen. She moaned and _____ when her _____ was stolen." (*Answers*: moped, moped.)

Setting Goals for Enjoying

Use goal setting to direct and enhance enjoying. Enjoyment can be spontaneous (e.g., suddenly finding the right answer). Students can also learn to set goals for bringing about enjoyment. Three things are helpful in goal setting for enjoyment in a school setting: the first is to identify in writing a goal that will bring personal enjoyment (ESL student wanting improvement in speaking English). The second is to recognize and list at least the high-profile conditions that help and hinder movement toward the goal (student's teacher taking a Spanish for Educators class; student having difficulty practicing English in teacher's lecture-oriented class). Sometimes it is worthwhile to identify who is involved in reaching the goal and a target date for reaching the goal. The third is to identify with the advice and consent of a teacher, coach, parent, or peer the level of enjoyment that will indicate achievement of the goal (student earning a desired minor role with dialogue in the school play). This level of attainment for the enjoyment can be verified personally if the goal is not being pursued officially for class credit or the like. Of course, achieving one enjoyment goal can lead to identifying and pursuing another, and enjoyment goals will need to be monitored by the teacher if a requirement is to keep them connected to the immediate or long-term class curriculum.

Guide and Follow-Up Questions for Teachers and Students

1. Do I work to help students extend their acts for potential enjoyment beyond the classroom—through homework assign-

ments, for example? This includes challenges for them in line with philosopher and economist John Stewart Mill's statement that "the pupil who is never required to do what he cannot do, will never do what he can do" (Young, 2004, p. 2).

2. Am I one who "bugs" the principal or the PTA or others to purchase or obtain for the teachers' lounge books and materials that extend knowledge for teaching the act of enjoying? One such book for studying the "enemy" of enjoying in order to increase ability to teach *for* enjoying is *Targeting Violence in Our Schools: Thinking Toward Solutions* by Brenda Guenther LeTendre and Richard P. Lipka (2003). Resources for collecting (sometimes free) material that can be used to challenge students with an intent to increase their overall enjoyment in learning are the U.S. Government cosponsored ERIC Clearinghouses. An example can be found at www.ael.org/ cress. Good resources on constructivism, the "father" of potential enjoyment in learning, are available through ASCD at www.ascd.org. Try *The Case for Constructivist Classrooms* (1993) by Jacqueline Grennon Brooks and Martin G. Brooks, for instance. Check also Sornson's *Teaching and Joy* (1996), edited by Robert Sornson. A good free resource is *Saudi Aramco World* with its articles such as *Zalabia and the First Ice-Cream Cone* (www.saudiaramcoworld.com; click on indexes, then subjects). The magazine educates on a culture perhaps unfamiliar to many students while at the same time offering a sense of enjoyment in learning. Another good and free resource for the lounge is the A&E Television Networks' *Idea Book for Educators*, available twice a year through AETV.com/ class.

3. Am I developing my skills for increasing enjoyment in my classroom? Do I consciously and on a regular basis practice "wait time" (e.g., giving myself sufficient time to reflect before responding to the individual constructions of my students and giving my students ample time—at least 3 seconds—to construct and offer their own meanings)? Do I consistently and objectively analyze and evaluate my procedures for teaching the act of enjoying? For instance, do I ask students to justify

and refine their constructions in order to strengthen or radically modify them? Do I apply rubrics or other measurement devices to cooperative learning endeavors in my classroom?

4. Have I subscribed to one or more professional magazines that can provide me with ideas and strategies for bringing more enjoyment into my teaching and for my students (e.g., *Instructor* at www.scholastic.com/instructor or *English Journal*)? For working with younger children, try *The Mailbox* or *Teaching PreK-8* at www.TeachingK-8.com.

TEACHING HUMAN RELATIONS IN THE CLASSROOM

Teaching human relations involves both teacher and students concentrating on the wonder of each individual and helping that person come increasingly more into full possession of his or her own particular powers in order to strike a point of harmony with self and the world, both in and out of the classroom. We can all continue to grow! To teach human relations in the classroom, teachers must believe that, not just say it. In the title words of the now classic 1962 *Association for Supervision and Curriculum Development Yearbook*, human relations teaching involves "perceiving, behaving, becoming" as done by *all* members of the classroom community. In classroom practice today, teaching human relations is most visible in multicultural education (diversity issues, discrimination, stereotyping) and in gender equity and sex-fair education. It incorporates lessons in classroom community building (establishing positive relationships as an alternative to bullying and name calling, working with students with disabilities), lessons dealing with how to function effectively in groups, and lessons in understanding and tolerating diverse sexual orientations.

Since the start of the war on terrorism, teaching human relations in the classroom has expanded to include increasing attention on partnering with parents, talking with students about tragedy and violence, discussing legal issues and responsibilities related to weapons and drugs possession, and dealing with peer pressure and conflict in and outside the classroom and the school. It has also revisited, and reemphasized, character education and the teaching of ethics, morals, and values. The most dominant value, for example, clearly operating in American education today is that of academic achievement ("Back to Basics"; "No one in my classroom who has really tried has ever gotten an F"). *What* values, morals, and ethics should be identified, clarified, and fostered by teachers who are clear, grounded but tolerant, and professional in their own way of operating is the primary question for those teaching the full scope of human relations, and for all teachers since teaching by its nature is a moral and value-based enterprise. Value-free education is a contradiction in terms. However, specific values, ethics, and morals for inclusion in the curriculum, to an appreciable extent, vary with the situation. Parents, curriculum specialists, and school authorities all need to be involved in the selection and in the teaching–learning process. Nonetheless, some generally accepted values, ethics, and morals, validated by the long run of school experience and even our American Constitution and Bill of Rights, can serve a benchmark function:

- It is important to consistently and carefully examine the repeated behaviors or life patterns of persons whose behaviors and life patterns are morally, ethically, to be preferred (Who demonstrated higher morals and ethics: Adolf Eichmann, a straight-A student in ethics at the University of Konigsberg or his contemporary who did poorly in the "basics" and failed the sixth grade—Winston Churchill?)

- It is important to be able to choose freely from alternatives and to be happy with the choice (this is generally preferable to yielding passively to authority or peer pressure).

- It is important to question, including asking questions of authority figures (questioning is a long-accepted value in American society, even our "Star-Spangled Banner" begins and ends with a question).

- Every person is precious in some way because he or she is unique.

- One should hold to personal courage in the face of pressure and be accountable for personal actions.

- It is important to strive to do good using honorable means.

- Self-discipline is critical to the life well lived.

- It is important to acquire and maintain respect for democratic principles such as freedom of speech, freedom of religion, and due process of law.

- It is important to be willing to publicly affirm and act on one's own morals, ethics, and values but to do so without detriment to oneself or others.

When teaching character education, ethics, morals, and values as part of teaching human relations in the classroom, teachers should remember that they, themselves, serve as role models of certain values, that it is reasonable to assume some connection between what and how young people are taught and how they behave, that in-class discussion of moral and ethical dilemmas can develop moral reasoning skills, that the main emphasis of teachers should be on helping students identify and sort through their emerging values, ethics, and morals—not on proselytizing or indoctrinating—and that this kind of education is compatible with teaching to the standards (e.g., in studying *Hamlet*, students could engage with the following ethical question: King Claudius supposedly killed to get ahead. How far would you go to get what you want?).

At the core of teaching human relations is demonstrating and building respect for oneself and one's potential and for others in all the major and minor events of classroom life. When teachers teach human relations in their classrooms, they become active observers, questioners, listeners, and readers (e.g., of what students write), *and* they trust their instincts. With human relations teaching, neither teachers nor students are expected to leave their feelings at the classroom door; they become a legitimate part of the instructional process. However, teachers are certainly more responsible for at least controlling their own emotions. In addition, teaching human relations by definition very much requires a teacher who understands *how students differ in their approaches to learning* and *creates instructional opportunities*, on a consistent basis, *that are adaptive to diverse learners* (INTASC principle 3). Within those opportunities, students are helped to identify their abilities, many of which are still unknown to them, and they are assisted to further understand, deepen, and control those abilities, at least some of them, given the academic learning time and resources available. In human relations teaching, the teacher is always the person primarily responsible for what takes place in the classroom, but that responsibility includes sharing power and facilitating students' growth in learning that some of their abilities and connected beliefs and behaviors, even those of which they are still becoming increasingly aware, are influencing their relationships with others.

Overall, teaching human relations in the classroom is a *doing* adventure. Teachers do "catch students doing good," for example, but in addition they are tough minded and require students to work up to increasingly high but realistic expectations or deal with the known consequences. The teacher teaching human relations is clearly responsible for creating a culture that holds students accountable for their behaviors. Diversity is celebrated in teaching human relations and intentionally and joyfully incorporated to enrich classroom learning. People are respected, but not necessarily their beliefs or behaviors. Prosocial skills are deliberately taught to help students proactively manage anger and impulsive and antisocial behaviors and to help them practice "refusal skills" and consciously internalize and practice empathy. In sum, if teachers want to have students and themselves working together as a community of scholars and collaborators to achieve success with the standards or other aspects of the academic curriculum, then they need to respect and care for one another, and that means teaching human relations in the classroom.

Work Options

The Valued "Cs"

Provide students with opportunities to engage with some valued "Cs" of classroom ethics, morality, and character education: careful choosing, courage, compassion, citizenship, (self) control, caring, craftsmanship/ commitment to excellence in school work, cooperation, and competence—in skills such as mathematics, reading, and research. An example from literature would be having students identify, consider, discuss, and weigh the choices Brutus has in Shakespeare's *Julius Caesar*. You and the students need not always agree when engaging with the "Cs"; the lasting learning may come from the recognition that all of us live continually immersed in a world of choices; that world is unavoidable and often difficult, but through this activity students can also learn to value it as a world to be welcomed.

Teaching Tolerance

With the help of volunteer students, find some human relations–connected music they appreciate and that you will listen to. In the search process, you may both come to understand and at least tolerate each other's musical choices. For example, a choice of our generation is "You've Got to Be Carefully Taught" from *South Pacific*. For today's high school students, a choice might be "Where Is the Love" by the Black Eyed Peas. For elementary students, choices could come from the excellent "I Will Be Your Friend" songbook, available free from the Southern Poverty Law Center at www.teachingtolerance.org. Play the music in class; discuss its message on tolerance, and let it lead into investigation of nontolerant or hate group rhetoric on the Internet (e.g., Aryan Nations, Ku Klux Klan). How are the arguments of these groups constructed? What faulty assumptions are embedded? Where does the logic fail? What are the purposes of these groups? What is the role of free speech regarding the messages of the hate groups? Is it possible to *not* tolerate the message while tolerating the messenger? When? This activity can carry over to homework and can enlist the guidance and support of parents.

Little Things

Little things do mean a lot when teaching human relations effectively in the classroom. Lots of little things can be done on a daily basis, directly and indirectly. For instance, you could model acceptance and reject put-downs of the different accents of your multicultural and multilingual students. You could teach a lesson on praise, helping students use deserved and appropriate praise with one another, praise that has specifics attached such as "Good hypothesis! The substance is acidic when it has a low pH." Teach praising that is not overdone but that is integrated within the larger context of showing respect for the person in the process of learning. You could also provide human relations challenges for students to do in their "free" time. These are generally completed without extensive teacher help, can be done in a fairly short amount of time, and are always available in the classroom. An example is designing a crossword puzzle of words and definitions related to diversity, culture, and gender stereotyping.

Examining Human Relations in Context

Identify with students some of the important learnings they now should have as a result of your last unit of academic instruction. Ask them to demonstrate their grasp of these learnings in a simulated meeting situation (e.g., the townspeople of Hamelin meeting with the Pied Piper, Galileo at his trial before the Inquisition in 1633, Benjamin Franklin cajoling from the French monarchy the aid and alliance to help America secure its independence). It makes good sense to provide meeting situations pertinent to your subject area(s), such as that of Galileo to mathematics or science, or Ben Franklin to social studies. In these situations, you can give students roles or just let them respond as themselves (e.g., a role in the Pied Piper situation could be that of a minority who is looking to see that equal attention is being paid to recovering the blind child and the mute child of Hamelin who were among the 130 led away by the piper's flute; another role could be that of the mayor of Hamelin). In the meeting, points may be earned by a student who offers up a concept learned in the unit, such as the use of estimation in mathematics (e.g., suggesting approximately how many dollars we would need today to meet the Pied Piper's fee in 1284 of 1,000 guilders) or one who makes an identifiable human relations behavior (e.g., offering to cooperate to find out why the piper's fee was not originally paid). You are the final awarder of points earned. A certain number of points equals an A; no points earned equals a D or F. (Teaching human relations includes accepting a student's choice to fail but giving continual help and opportunities so that failure is not the preferred choice.) At the conclusion of this performance exam, debrief with the students: What were their feelings? Did they see how the academic content they studied plays into real life? Do applied human relations behaviors help solve problems? What does it mean today to "pay the piper"?

Observing "Real" Human Relations

Locate, perhaps with student help, some notable "literary lies" for treatment in upcoming oral and/or written composition assignments in

English/language arts. Some examples include Topsy's storytelling in Harriet Beecher Stowe's *Uncle Tom's Cabin* (2004), the two boys misrepresenting themselves to everyone in Mark Twain's *The Prince and the Pauper* (1881), Twain's Huck Finn trying to convince the riverside lady that he was a girl in order to protect his black friend, and Arbatan in *Story of the Other Wise Man* by Henry van Dyke (1996) standing in the doorway of the little cottage in Bethlehem and telling a lie to turn Herod's men from the bloody slaughter of the child within. Stimuli for composition could include the following questions: Are such lies ever justifiable? Are they a mark of low ethical standards or poor moral character? Are they better than the alternative? Are they an inevitable part of human relations? Identifying and dealing with "lies" in other areas of academic instruction—math, social studies, science—makes for a worthwhile human relations teaching and learning activity. So does having students view stories or film that are basically true, such as the movie *Bridge on the River Kwai*. This picture portrays conditions that make ethical principles impractical or painful to abide by or at least open to question. Students could role-play the main characters and discuss forthcoming questions about the actions of one man, Colonel Nicholson, who had a direct effect on the lives and well-being of a group of prisoners. What moral right did he have to decide the fate of others? Does the moral code of behavior by which we live in a civilian life carry over into extreme situations such as war? Nicholson strongly values his own refusing to compromise. When does such strong "valuing" become egotism or fanaticism and get in the way of effective human relations?

Quoting Human Relations

Find some quotes by important people that are pertinent to human relations. Discuss, perhaps in student trios, or post the quotes around the classroom along with written student interpretations, agreements, disagreements, and *student* quotes (they are important people) as well. If you can find quotes in your own discipline(s), that often adds academic relevance to the activity.

Here are some examples:

"Every morning upon awakening, I experience a supreme pleasure: that of being Salvador Dali, and I ask myself, wonder-

struck, what prodigious thing will he do today."—Salvador
Dali, Spanish surrealist artist (*art*)

"So in every individual the two trends, one towards personal happiness and the other towards unity with the rest of humanity,
must contend with each other."—Sigmund Freud, Austrian
psychologist (*psychology*)

"Man's inhumanity to man makes countless thousands mourn."—
Robert Burns, Scottish poet (*English*)

"All religions must be tolerated, and the sole concern of the
authorities should be to see that one does not molest another,
for here every man must be saved in his own way."—
Frederick the Great, King of Prussia (*social studies*)

"Love is the ability to communicate by demonstrative acts to others our profound involvement in their welfare."—Ashley
Montagu, American anthropologist (*science*)

Cooperative Learning

Some evidence suggests that cooperative learning activities, when
properly conducted, promote higher levels of well-adjusted social relations
and basic trust in and optimism about people when compared with com-
petitive and individualistic situations. So, take a risk and try some cooperative learning activities with students. For example, have class teams
prepare a meaningful proposal for public audiences such as the school
principal or the parent–teacher association on why their school needs air-
conditioning. Or, ask teams to investigate, study, and report to the class
on different parts of the current academic curriculum.

Guide and Follow-Up Questions for Teachers and Students

1. Am I aware of organizations that offer, often for free, excellent
   materials and ideas for teaching human relations? These
   include the Character Education Partnership, a national coali-
   tion providing principles and resources for development of
   character education in public schools (www.character.org).
   Another is the Southern Poverty Law Center with their free,

to educators, magazine *Teaching Tolerance* (www.toler-ance.org). Giant Brands, Inc., now puts out an excellent *Pro-files in Excellence* pamphlet; free class sets of each issue can be obtained for teaching multicultural education. Issue 11 (2003), for instance, celebrates African American heritage. Giant Food's Office of Minority Affairs is at 301-341-4740, or log onto www.giantfood.com.

2. What statements, comments, or beliefs do I, or my students or their parents, know—or can locate or invent—that could be used to decorate the classroom and to challenge everyone continually about the meaning and importance of human rela-tions? Here are some: "Character consists of what you do on the 3rd and 4th tries," James A. Michener, American writer; "To be able to practice five things everywhere under heaven constitutes perfect virtue. . . . [They are] gravity, generosity of soul, sincerity, earnestness and kindness," Confucius, Chinese philosopher; "I hold that while man exists it is his duty to improve not only his own condition but to assist in ameliorat-ing mankind," Abraham Lincoln, American politician; "Everything that enlarges the sphere of human powers, that shows man he can do what he thought he could not do, is val-uable," Dr. Samuel Johnson, English lexicographer; "Never one thing and seldom one person can make for a success. It takes a number of them merging into one perfect whole," Marie Dressler, American actress. Students should be invited to draw appropriate illustrations, with credit to the student artist, to accompany these ideas and thereby make them into pieces of classroom art.

3. Are we, here in our classroom (teacher and student), *really* willing to identify and challenge our own bias and prejudices when it comes to other people? Are we willing to look at oth-ers for something in common within our cultural backgrounds, ethnicity, individual experiences, and personal values? Are we willing to judge people as individuals and not just as represen-tatives of groups? Can we shift our own points of view to establish relationships with those who *don't* share our beliefs? Can we accept the bottom line reality—with its corresponding

responsibilities—that in human relations, love and respect of
self is necessary for generating legitimate love of others? Are
we willing and tough minded enough to make this classroom
truly a place where effective human relations is consistently
practiced within an environment that creates space for individual differences? These questions could be the subject of prean-
nounced class meetings in which the teacher joins the students
in a circle and is a contributing member.

4. Do I, as probably the person in the classroom most legally and
professionally responsible for practicing teaching, objectively
check myself on a continual basis to be sure that I am giving
sufficient and relatively equal opportunities for both boys and
girls to be called on and participate in learning activities that
appeal sometimes perhaps more to girls, sometimes more to
boys, and sometimes to both sexes? (A class roster with tally
marks or a simple event log could help.) Do I, in general,
model effective human relations with the "7Ps" with whom I
come into continual contact as a professional teacher: my
peers, principals (administrators, supervisors), the public,
pupils, professionals (guidance counselors, ESL resource
teachers), parents, and my private self.

5. To what commitment of my time and energy am I willing to
do follow-up work on human relations? Examples: Check into
finding likely root causes for human relations behaviors (desirable and undesirable); surf the web; read *Stop the Bullying: A
Handbook for Schools* by Ken Rigby (2001). Search out symptoms or indications of human relations behaviors (invite, not
require, students to share journals—they may even talk about
suicide). Write letters to individual students with an evaluation of their skills in human relations; offer suggestions for
improvement and why improvement might be wise for that
individual. And, will I pursue my own intellectual growth in
this area of teaching human relations, such as reading about
Lawrence Kohlberg's six stages of moral development as found
in educational foundation texts such as the seventh edition of
Teachers, Schools, and Society by Myra Pollack Sadker and
David Miller Sadker (2005)?

TEACHING POSITIVE SELF-CONCEPT

Self-concept is the mental image (perceptions, feelings, attitudes) a student has of himself or herself, formed in great part by what the student thinks *others* think of him or her. It is the way students describe themselves based on the roles they play and the personal attributes they think they possess. Since roles and attributes change, self-concept is in a constant state of flux; in fact, students not only carry images of the self in several areas (academic achiever, helpful peer, "goof-off") but also possess the potential for developing many more (what he or she would like to be). Direct teaching for positive, healthy, realistic self-concept is a significant, if not necessarily causal, factor for helping students enhance their academic performance; it is imperative for helping students learn to make sound choices and commitments, follow through with them, and stand up independently in the classroom and the world as good learners and good people. A reference from the Talmud speaks to the importance of self-concept: "We do not see things as they are; we see things as we are."

Self-esteem is the crucial measurement component of self-concept. Self-esteem is how students evaluate themselves and their characteristics; it is their personal judgment of their worthiness. For example, holding high respect for oneself as a competent follower can be just as revealing of a realistic, positive self-concept as can viewing oneself as a classroom leader. The job of teachers working with self-esteem is to help students validate their judgment of their own worthiness and help them make accurate assessments of themselves so they can make necessary changes in continuing to mature in integrity, responsibility, and achievement.

In classroom practice, teachers enhance student self-concept by showing appreciation of the students' worth (not necessarily beliefs or behaviors) by finding, for example, one thing each student can do well—his or her "islands of competence"—and looking for opportunities to allow the student to use that ability; holding high but realistic expectations and informing students of these (expect the possible—turning a paper in on time—not the impossible); making discipline and management moves in a supportive manner (with courtesy and firmness reject the act, not the child); helping pupils develop appreciation of their own cultural heritage (add a cultural item to the classroom for making a more attractive learning environment); and giving students genuine responsibility and opportunity to assist in developing, carrying out, and evaluating (some) lessons in the curriculum.

Building positive, healthy self-concept basically emphasizes providing positive encounters in the classroom. Students read well the signals sent to them from those in their environment. When teachers invite a computer literate student to discuss with the class how to do PowerPoint presentations, it gives that student a feeling of being prized, encourages him or her to live up to the teacher's expectations ("Pygmalion" in the classroom), and increases the likelihood of a positive self-image. Healthy self-concept may also be increased by student growth in recognizing *negatives* in the classroom climate (constant criticism) and finding the psychological strength for choosing nonviolent options such as subsequently hiding or redirecting feelings. Here, the positive growth comes in appreciating one's own ability to correctly recognize a problem and solve it even though a possible outcome of less interaction with the teacher, for instance, may be held in question. Positive self-concept may be enhanced by teacher actions through helping students meet their need to belong, nurturing them in their own personal capabilities for doing some thing(s) at least reasonably well, and helping them validate and refine their sense of individual worth as ongoing and capable learners. Student self-concept is always part of what a teacher affects, intentionally or indirectly, when he or she *plans instruction based upon knowledge of subject matter, students, the community, and curriculum goals* (INTASC principle 7).

In sum, when teaching positive self-concept, teachers are working consciously in the outer space of the classroom with the inner space of each student, the self-concept. Moreover, that work is directed toward helping each student appraise himself or herself accurately. With teaching self-concept, the question often arises that students can get a naïve or inflated opinion of themselves even with teacher guidance, too much of "I am the king of the kingdom of me." True! Perhaps Shakespeare's comment in *Henry V*, Act II, Scene 4, offers an applicable response to this concern: "Self love, my liege, is not so vile a sin as self neglecting." Building positive self-concept through high expectations and effective pedagogical practices may account to an appreciable degree for school success in standards and other areas of academic life—and gains in scholarly competence may often *precede* increases in self-concept. What is desired overall is a positive, healthy self-image that includes a realistic assessment and acceptance of one's unique *self* in all its dimensions, combined with a recognition of how individual strengths and limitations can be adapted to actually succeed in a responsible life.

Work Options

Increasing Awareness of Incidental Learnings

An incidental learning is one that was probably *not* intended by the sender for others to pick up. It is usually presented without conscious awareness on the part of the sender, and it may have a positive, negative, or neutral effect on a receiver's self-concept. To increase awareness of incidental learnings, play an audio- or videotape or show a school poster, community announcement, or commercial advertisement and identify with the students some incidental learnings they received. Treat these learnings as follows: What was the incidental learning? What caused the incidental learning? What was the learning probably intended to accomplish? What could be done to generate the building of positive self-concept from the situation?

Here is an example:

School poster—*Do well in the state tests!*

Incidental learning—"The true and final purpose of *my* education here is to give my school a strong reputation with the state."

Analysis and revision—"I guess the poster meant well for getting us thinking about the upcoming tests, but I would feel better about myself if I thought my role here was not just to be used by the school for their 'feel good' purposes, but that I was really valued by the school for myself." The poster could be accompanied by administrative announcements saying that study sessions will be available for interested students and that they will be run primarily to answer student questions in different academic areas.

Learning From High Expectations

To be effective in developing positive self-concept, think of at-risk students—and all students—as being "at promise." Holding high expectations for these at-promise students in discipline and academics can lead to high achievement as, over time, students generally live up to teachers' expectations. As they continue to have success with the high and realistic expectations, their image of themselves as a classroom success will grow. One example: Ask low-achieving students to teach others in the class about a personal interest or to demonstrate a unique skill or talent as it relates to some academic study in the curriculum. Remember, as you hold students to high expectations for helping them develop positive self-concept, you will *increase* the differences in your classroom. (Students who believe in their own capacities and have the courage—and help—to achieve them will separate themselves from others with different capacities. Students are not universally uniform in their talents; living with such increasing disparity in the classroom requires strong self-concept on the part of teachers.)

Researching Self-Concept Theory

Invite student research papers on self-concept theory. Point out to students the objectives of these electronic or hard-copy papers are to increase ability to produce research papers, to learn more about self-concept, and to apply what is learned toward better understanding of their own self-concept. In this activity, analysis precedes modification; as students research and examine self-concept theory and reflect on what they learn, they may well build more personally positive self-concept through success with the process, as well as from the information gained. One theory (Canfield & Wells, 1976) is the "poker chip theory," which holds that each student's self-concept is analogous to a stack of poker chips. Some students have a lot of chips to use in the learning game; they have enjoyed prior academic successes, for instance. Others have fewer chips because of learning failures, substance abuse, and the like. The students with many chips can take risks for learning, can even risk losing a bit of his or her self-concept. Students with few chips may be reluctant to risk rejection in the learning process. They may withdraw from the game: "This is stupid!

I won't do it." (Translation: "I'm afraid I can't do it.") The job of significant others in the learning community—teachers, parents, friends—is to
help students build up enough chips to at least stay in the game. Ultimately, each student should figure out how to replenish and add to his or
her own supply of chips for independent and successful learning.

Students of appropriate age could also research adolescent development theories. For instance, a well-discussed belief about girls is that for
them adolescence is a watershed with a potential drop in psychological
resilience and an increase in concern about their body image and their
degree of social acceptance, all of which impact on their developing an
increasingly negative or positive self-concept. Or, students could research
crosscultural theories on self-concept. In Japanese elementary schools, for
example, self-concept is not so much separate identity but more a concept
that places at the center of personal development the self *and* a few inti-
mate others. This belief in group harmony helps define self-concept while
encouraging each student to offer some (probably different) special talent
to the learning enterprise, thereby bringing the child to more positive feeling about himself or herself. In Malaysia and Indonesia, the idea of self-
concept embraces emotions; interestingly, the emotional center of the body
is considered to be not the heart, as it is in Western culture, but the liver!

Building Positive Self-Concept Through "Quickies"

On a regular basis, give students short activities for developing positive
self-concept. Participate in them yourself, and place them in a nurturing,
affective climate. No grades will be attached to the activities, but students
might be encouraged to keep a confidential journal on their thoughts about
their own changing self-concept. A good source for "quickie" material is
The Mailbox: The Idea Magazine for Teachers. Others are *Early Childhood
Today* (www.early childhoodtoday.com) and *Instructor*'s arts and crafts supplement from Crayola (www.scholastic.com/instructor). *Note:* See if your
principal or PTA would order these magazines for teachers to use. When
working with "quickies," concentrate on what the activity is and how it
works; how it might be used, as adapted, to build healthy self-concept; how
its success might be evaluated; and what ethical considerations should be
kept in mind when using this activity.

Here is an example:

Commercial for oneself—Tell students to make an advertisement for any desired media outlet (TV, magazine, billboard, merchandising coupon, school paper) in order to sell themselves. They could work with other students in preset classroom time. Results may be shared with the entire class without prizes or winners.

Success symbols—Have students bring to class a tangible object that symbolizes some past success or accomplishment on their part. These are shared with the class on a voluntary basis to include associated feelings and comments on the success symbolized.

Boast roast—Point to any student and ask that student to stand up and name a classmate to boast about, making sure to identify that student by name. The speaker must make one or two complimentary statements about whomever he or she chooses. *That* student, in turn, picks another classmate to so honor. Eventually every student gets a chance to boast and to be boasted about in a supportive, positive, kind, and constructive manner.

Hanging pride—Students select a string of colored yarn and hang it from the ceiling over their desks. They attach to the string a favorite piece of work from the day or week. Everyone always has something on display for the period of the activity. As these hangings change over time, growing student maturity, competence, and positive self-confidence is also measured.

Learning From Low, Medium, and High Self-Concept Examples

Encourage students to locate examples of different levels of self-concept. These can be located in a variety of formats (poetry, newspaper human interest stories, film) and brought to class and discussed. Examples from poetry: "Willy Wet-Leg" by D. H. Lawrence (low); "Aedh Wishes for the Cloths of Heaven" by W. B. Yeats (medium); "The Mouse That Gnawed the Oak-Tree Down" by Vachel Lindsay (individual high); and "Ourchestra" by Shel Silverstein (group high). For extreme "low" examples, try Woody Allen's old film, *Zelig*, in which Woody portrays a character who changed his appearance, personality, and behavior, even his race or nationality, to resemble whomever he was with. (By transforming himself to be exactly like other people, Zelig hoped he would be loved and accepted.) For very "high," check Astrid Lindgren's *Pippi Longstocking* and Pippi's conversation with her teacher on her first day in a new school.

Conferencing Challenges

Invite students to *lead* a parent–teacher conference involving their own parent(s). Shortly after the conference, which has been agreed to by parents, be sure to give all participants an opportunity to provide feedback concerning the effectiveness of the student-led format so the model can be fine-tuned. When done appropriately, with adequate preparation of students (organizational and communication skills), the teacher serving as facilitator, sample questions provided for parents to ask their children, and a few private minutes reserved at the end for a traditional parent–teacher talk, this can *really* build positive student self-concept.

Guide and Follow-Up Questions for Teachers and Students

1. Am I as their teacher willing to set up at my desk a teacher expectations chart that will help me develop healthy, positive self-concept with my students? (See figure 12.1.)

Student(s) Present Behavior	My Negative Expectations	My Positive Expectations for Building Healthy Self-Concept	Actions to Bring About Column 3
Tarry, 3rd period, does not do what I ask	She is apathetic and will get an F	She has an *independent* mind	Give more *clarity* to my directions, and check with Tarry

Figure 12.1   Teacher Expectations Chart

2. How do I answer this very pertinent question: Is it very important for teachers to help all students experience success in one way or another outside of the prescribed academic curriculum? Why or why not? (Also, a yes/no student debate to include the possible dominance of standards could be held on this issue.)

3. How can I, as the teacher, show students and parents I value building positive self-concept? For example would I be willing to add, with comment, a grade for the reporting period on self-concept (e.g., math, B; science, B; social studies, A; language arts, C; self-concept, B)?

4. Can I come up with ways to measure self-concept, to get at self-esteem? A simple checklist developed with teacher advisement and with items rated by students (1 to 5, 5 being highest) according to their present judgment is an example. (See figure 12.2.)

How I See Myself   How I'd Like to Be

_____   I understand myself.   _____

_____   I am a failure.   _____

_____   I am a good sport.   _____

_____   I do well on tests.   _____

_____   I can't . . .   _____

Figure 12.2   Checklist to Measure Self-Concept

5. Am I willing to pursue professional learning in the area of self-concept, looking at the very pertinent materials available from Jalmar Press, www.jalmarpress.com, for instance? Or analyzing my teaching practices (such as asking for and using student suggestions or encouraging sensible risk taking) using videotape or a colleague coach to see if I behave consistently in ways, for example, that make my appropriate expectations about students more likely to be fulfilled—and revising those that might lead to students' continuing negative self-concept, such as my student saying "I don't really need plastic surgery,

but I will get it to be better accepted by the teacher and the other girls."

6. What can be done in my classroom to create high, healthy, positive, realistic self-concept for all students? Reflect on this with parents and students and take appropriate action. Example: Create a climate characterized by the building blocks of warmth (students are important and enjoyable people and deserve to feel welcome and be taken seriously in the classroom, not to be embarrassed or put down); student interactive participation in decision making; flexibility in grouping (not always by ability); emphasis on success (provide attainable goals and learning opportunities that take into account individual differences and aptitudes, and acknowledge success with honest feedback); encouragement of students to pursue activities they find appealing and meaningful—even challenging—but might be hesitant to try; teaching students to analyze and evaluate their own progress; and inclusion of curriculum, with parental involvement when possible, that pays attention to continuing personal and social development (even with anticipation, clearly defined limits, and correction, mistakes are still an inevitable and acceptable part of the ongoing healthy self-concept growth process). Don't forget to *model* positive, optimistic, and professional self-concept with its attention to listening, learning, respect, competence, and caring; let it connect as it will to building student self-concept.

TEACHING SERVICE EDUCATION

Teaching service education, or preparing students for community service, means creating a classroom community—usually in a middle or high school—with a service mind-set. It means fulfilling a genuine community need while maintaining a viable connection to academic content. When school learning is connected through a helping relationship to life outside school, students are often more increasingly motivated and committed to learning. They can, for example, in the "outside" world come into contact with possible careers that predominantly use math or science or English and which increase their attention to one or more of those subjects in school. In teaching service education effectively, both the teacher and the students work as a team through a shared commitment to making a positive contribution to the larger world than the classroom. In this process of enriching lives, students ultimately evolve as responsible, resourceful members of their neighborhoods and communities. They demonstrate an understanding of the relationship between their immediate environment (school) and their community heritage and realities and how the interaction between the two shapes and impacts their lives. Community service programs allow students to develop life skills as they battle with very real local and even global issues, assume new responsibilities, explore new roles, face new challenges, and learn how to interact productively and socialize positively with the larger society in which they are integrated. Teachers who choose to teach service education incorporate the following in their instruction:

- Selecting collaborative projects that challenge and stretch students cognitively and developmentally. Students may also suggest their own interventions with which their strengths are well matched

- Requiring application of concepts, content, and skills from the academic disciplines while recognizing students' abilities and limitations

- Engaging all students (not just "gifted and talented") with authentic service projects that have clear goals or meet genuine needs in the community and for which students (and others) will share realistic expectations

- Soliciting significant student voice in project selection, design, implementation, and evaluation

- Preparing students in advance, and during the task, for the project and its success (e.g., previewing safety rules)

- Supervising student work, including monitoring their ethical and confidential treatment of information discovered during the service project (e.g., use of illegal drugs)

- Incorporating reflection and sharing of observations and insights and individual learnings before, during, and after the service project

- Promoting ongoing communication with all involved with the project

- Acknowledging, celebrating, and validating students' work inside and outside the school environment

- Using assessment tools to document student learning and the outcomes of the service project (e.g., portfolios, time sheets, rating summaries, and task progress reports by supervisors)

- Helping students predict how what they learned can provide guidance for their future

Contemporary service education evolved out of the National and Community Service Act signed into law in November 1990 by President George Bush to promote service learning activities to young people. In its definition, it goes beyond performing a legitimate task through community service or volunteering (making gifts for shut-in people) to include a teaching and learning methodology in which young people learn and develop civic responsibility through actively meeting community needs, in collaboration with schools and communities and through school curricula. Students examine data, think critically and creatively, use communication skills, confront diversity, and contribute to effective problem solving. Service education, to illustrate, involves helping care for others by making playgrounds safer, using academic skills and knowledge to work productively with the homeless, extending personal learning in breadth (and depth) beyond the prescribed in-school curriculum (investigating the psychology behind hate graffiti on religious buildings), and reflecting on the activities and learning experienced. In service education projects, middle and high school students might "adopt" senior citizens, take on local ecology projects, tutor homebound students, help address public health issues, and aid the hungry and homeless. Service education students work alone and in groups to identify problems and come up with reasonable solutions.

On the cautionary side of service education, students are often only chasing their hour requirement for community service to graduate or retain their National Junior Honor Society (NJHS) membership. Many students, and teachers, end up viewing community service as doing a few sporadic activities to graduate or as a one-time special event. Teachers feel pressed for time, and in their endeavor to complete curriculum standards and guidelines, they sometimes approach service projects with trepidation. In fully teaching service education, teachers need to understand that integrating community service into their teaching exposes students to different learning experiences outside the class or school and gives them a new identity as "citizens." Students as citizens not only engage in the active process of problem solving and meaningful reflection but also act to become connected with their neighborhoods and communities. When they engage in service projects, students ask real-life questions, analyze the political and social climate of their communities, explore neighborhood issues that impact their present and future, and possibly even initiate a movement for positive change. When a teacher integrates projects with related moral, social, political, and civic issues into the curriculum, each student is able to make connections with the complicated realities of the outside world. This can lead students to develop concrete strategies for addressing issues they strongly care about and feel deeply about—and adds another dimension to their learning. Teaching service education especially from an integrated approach requires planning *instruction based upon knowledge of subject matter, students, the community, and curriculum goals* (INTASC principle 7).

At the bottom line, service education clearly requires understanding and appreciation of individual and community uniqueness. Students may team together and pool their talents to explore service learning projects in their immediate neighborhood: "Maybe we can help our local homeless shelter to assist persons living in their cars. We will send over our very courteous service team member, Kim, to check how we might begin working together with the shelter to learn more about the conditions of homelessness and to make a positive difference for the homeless in our community." When students begin to go outside themselves and become less self-absorbed, they get exposed to new experiences and learnings. These, when rooted outside their school existence, may help them better appreciate others and themselves. When students view the world in a fresh way, they often gain a fresh understanding of it and themselves and can perhaps better empathize with other people's points of view and feelings. Sharing community service experiences helps students learn to understand each other and live together more effectively. Working with different kinds of people with different personalities; handling different kinds of relationships; and sharing experiences, understanding, feelings, and opinions enables students to discover their unique talents and to, overall, build a sense of belonging.

In sum, service education is a desire in the teacher to use a different "textbook" (the community) for instruction in order to help students improve in academics (and foster a desire in students to strengthen their academic background), become better citizens by providing a positive contribution to their neighborhood, and reaffirm their understanding and appreciation of community values about the reciprocal connection between school and society. When students interact with others outside the classroom, they learn that they are not static and that others, too, go through this process of "becoming." And, in this process, students learn to reflect on and take action on community issues, speak up, and try on their earned role as newly responsible citizens. It might accurately be stated that the unofficial motto of service education is "One way for people to be greater than they are is to serve!"

Work Options

Building Strong Communities

Have students team together. When students share responsibilities in group activities, they learn to be responsible and accountable for their actions. Teaming together is the first step to develop a sense of community and an equitable community of learners. The following activities are targeted at building communities where everyone's contribution is valued.

Ask students to create a one-page advertisement for their talents. Display the advertisements on a board in the class. Then if a student needs help, he or she can consult the advertisements to find another student who can help with the specific need.

Read *The Giving Tree* by Shel Silverstein (1999). Conduct a literature circle and designate different roles to students to discuss the concept of giving. Discuss giving from the point of view of the tree and the boy. Divide the class into small groups and ask them to create pictures showing the things they give to their community and the things they receive from their community. Students can respond in their journals to the following prompts: "What action must I take to build community partnerships?" "What is teamwork?" "What skills of mine can help mobilize a service project?"

To arrive at a better understanding of the terms *volunteering* and *community resources*, students can write a report on a community member who is their role model, write brief biographies of people who play an important role in their communities, read current news and articles about their communities, create a collage of community workers, role-play different scenarios about serving the community, or make presentations to the school community on the positive aspects of contributing to a local community.

Students in Action

Conduct action projects. Action projects feed out of reflective practice. They are conducted in a practical real world of a classroom wherein the student examines issues that hold a potential for positive change.

Action projects foster stronger communities and bond the students with their communities through meaningful service. Students give voice to their own ideas for social change and identify school problems and issues such as bullying, drugs, or violence. For action projects, have students develop a plan, goals, objectives, and guidelines in collaboration with teachers, counselors, and the administration to address the issues. As a last step, reflect and evaluate the effectiveness of the project through surveys and interviews.

Brainstorm possible initiating service learning opportunities, which can span from meals on wheels for senior citizens to creating websites to keep the public informed of important community issues and trends to decorating a community bulletin board with environmental information. Let the students brainstorm and develop a "wish list" for group goals and a timeline to reach each goal. Then plan a team to make a tangible difference in a community. Remember, a good team is a culmination of people with a range of skills, expertise, and relationships to the community. It would help to ask students to reflect on these questions: How do we want our community to be impacted by our action? How will this action make our community a better place? What assets (funds, human resources, space, equipment) are available to us? What steps are required to achieve our goals? What are the possible roadblocks we might face? Six months from now, what will be different in the community as a result of our team efforts? A few project ideas generated by the students might include delivering newspapers, volunteering as a tour guide for a museum, organizing a safety watch event, reading stories at the library, organizing events to benefit youth organizations, informing local officials of a neighborhood safety issue, organizing a park clean-up, and visiting a nursing home or assisted living community and organizing games for patrons or entertaining them with skits, songs, and poetry reading. Students might also adopt a highway, sell popcorn and soup in the teacher's school cafeteria to raise money for a local charity, organize a fashion show, and assist the librarian with record keeping or ordering of materials and in-house accounting. In addition, students could correspond with local, state, or U.N. officials on relevant community, national, and international issues; organize recycling events; join an environmental group to rescue endangered species/rainforests/oceans; run a campaign on environmental issues; volunteer at an animal shelter or zoo; join a group or organization supporting world peace;

and correspond via e-mail with students from other countries on the issue of drugs and violence.

Online Resources

Use the Internet. For example, www.servenet.org. offers multiple volunteer opportunities for students. To access a list of opportunities, students need to enter their zip codes in the Get Involved search box. America's Promise, an organization that came into being in 1997 as a result of the U.S. presidents coming together in Philadelphia and declaring five promises that must be fulfilled for all children and youth, works in close collaboration with communities, schools, and partner organizations—including NASC, NHS, NJHS, and NASSP—to establish constructive alliances with the youth of America. For detailed information visit www.americaspromise.org. Visit www.nslexchange.org to access a national network of volunteer educators with experience and expertise in service learning. The educators provide their technical advice free of charge. The Learn and Serve America Grants Program is an integration program that links service learning programs with academic skills. Online grant applications for national and community service are available at www.nationalservice.org/egrants/index.html. In recognition for outstanding service to the community (50 or more hours of community service within a 12-month period) students can receive the President's Student Service Award and Scholarship. For details, visit www.student-service-awards.org. Free the Children offers ongoing projects to students to learn about cultural diversity and tolerance while helping other kids. For information about launching a project, visit www.freethechildren.org/youthinaction/projects_2004_2005.htm.

Peer to Peer

Plan student–student service relationships. Young people are working together today to initiate change in the lives of their peers. In an energized collective movement, students across the country have found innovative ways to voice their concerns about smoking, drugs, gang pressure, and violence. As role models to a generation of easily swayed peers, they can mentor, coach, and lead their peers to discover constructive ways to express themselves. Students can team together to raise awareness in their school and community about the dangers of drunk and drugged driving. To find out how to help a friend who drinks or does drugs, students can visit Freevibe.com. Students can campaign against hate crimes, bullying, drugs, teen pregnancies, and violence. They can peer tutor special needs students by reading to them, sharing their notes, helping them access electronic resources, and teaching them to organize their materials. Students can participate in a negotiation process with peers, serve as peer mediators in a classroom or a schoolwide program, engage in group problem-solving discussions, facilitate consensus decision making as a member of a group, or even coach younger students and peers to become expert peer mediators.

Simple Deeds

Involve students in service relationships. This approach works well with elementary grade students who are more spontaneous and less reticent about sharing details about their personal lives. Ask the students to make a list of simple things each one of them could do for others. Start with home activities, then expand the list to include friends and the neighborhood. Ask them to start a good deeds log with two columns. In the left column ask them to record their good deeds, and in the right column ask them to explain the feeling they experienced. After a week ask the students to share their logs with a partner and create a Venn diagram for feelings. Compile the feelings into a vocabulary list. Ask the students to select 10 words from the list and create a crossword puzzle using crossword-generating software. Elementary grade students can also create a "responsibility collage" with pictures from magazines showing people performing constructive tasks. Tie up this work option with a lesson on what it takes to be a good citizen. Students could begin to create their own "citizenship flowers" on a board, which would be linked to the new responsibility tasks they choose to perform at school and at home. Each petal could signify a good deed. Ask students to respond to this Japanese proverb: "To the world you may be someone, but to someone, you may be the world." Their reflections can be followed by a structured discussion on the potential in people to make a difference and change the world.

Planning for Service Education

Fill out a service education worksheet with students, and refer to it frequently during the service learning project. Be flexible in making

121

adjustments to it. Following are some questions that can be addressed on the worksheet:

- Who are we (class and teacher identification)?

- What is the type of our service activity and our beginning date?

- What are some of the significant needs in our community?

- In what order should these needs be prioritized?

- What is needed to get started on the number-one priority (e.g., resources, transportation, money)?

- Who, specifically, can help? What general groups can help" (e.g., local firemen)?

- What kind of training is needed (e.g., skills and information)?

- How can we get others involved (recruitment)?

- How should we inform the communities involved (e.g., newspapers)?

- What should be our plan (goals, timeline, initial procedures, evaluation techniques)?

- What did participants learn during the activity (answered individually)?

- How can we use what we learned in our "back home" academic environment?

- What other comments should be noted about this service project? Is it one worth doing again? Why or why not?

Guide and Follow-Up Questions for Teachers and Students

1. Do I recognize conflict as an inevitable part of community service? Teachers influence the attitudes of their students toward conflict resolution. Ask the following questions to understand your own conflict resolution aptitude: Do I express anger in a

positive and constructive way? Do I speak calmly without raising my voice and yelling? Do I listen to the point of view of the student, which may help in reframing the conflict, before giving my verdict? Do I negotiate to arrive at a mutual compromise? Do I summarize the cause of conflict and deal with it in a nonjudgmental way?

2. How far am I willing to go to demonstrate a sense of solidarity with the students? Teachers need to mobilize their students to improve the communities around them and support them to become responsible, enthusiastic, and empathetic contributors to the well-being of their communities. When teachers decide to be an active part of their students' service drive, the results are faster. Teachers can work in collaboration with the administration to set up an extrinsic reward system for the students to participate in schoolwide projects. Some examples include setting guidelines for earning points toward homework passes, treating the class with the highest targets achieved to a breakfast or a pizza treat, or dressing in different colors or even dyeing your hair to celebrate a fund-raising project.

3. Do I look for any relationship between service learning and academic performance? Are students who participate in service programs more driven? Do they find multiple opportunities in the course of the project to enhance their critical thinking skills, self-efficacy, and leadership ability?

4. Do I seek out ideas from the community for service projects that might interest my students? For example, local radio stations may have ideas—or the YMCA or community religious organizations.

TEACHING CREATIVE THINKING

Whether they are going to grow up to run an advertising campaign for Coke or Pepsi, or work on a cure for cancer, or write a Broadway play, or serve as a peacemaker to the world's wars, or, more realistically for most, whether they will help make their classroom a better facilitative environment for learning, or develop their own internal "crap detector" for use against the temptations and problems that constantly bombard them, or invent solutions for the junior class fundraisers, or become a community activist after graduation, students will need to think efficiently and effectively, critically and creatively—and doing so is not a widespread current reality for many students or their parents. In today's world—and for problem solving for a decent future— thinking critically and creatively is a necessity. Professional teachers can not allow students to echo King Arthur's plaintive cry for answers through magic: "Merlin, make me a hawk, so I can fly away."

Although current neuroscience research indicates aspects of thinking may well be inherent in the structure of the human brain—the left hemisphere especially associated with critical thinking and the right hemisphere more with creative thinking—teachers still need to bring thinking processes to consciousness and have students practice to improve them. Tactical intelligence (i.e., applied thinking) is not a natural thing. But with increased, supervised practice and experience, students are likely to move to a level at which their thinking is not slow, fumbling, and awkward but increasingly more sophisticated and quick. It usually requires much less cognitive energy—and probably time—to pull up a workable decision on a problem if a student has had a lot of consistent and teacher-planned experience with thinking and its component skills. Thinking, defined generically for instructional purposes, is the active process of stimulation and elaboration of cues in the mind in order to establish relationships with personal meanings. Its end product is physical and/or intellectual and/or emotional activity through which students attempt to master their bodies, their feelings, their problems, and their environments.

The process of thinking, pertinent to teaching, breaks into two fundamental categories: critical (logical, linear, rational, sequential) thinking and creative (lateral, divergent, intuitive, abstract) thinking. Both are needed—logical thinking, by itself, could become just a systematic way of arriving at the wrong answers. Critical thinking and creative thinking have much in common. Both, for instance, go across the school curriculum; both require cognitive skills such as observing, applying, and making connections; both rely on constructing and reconstructing personal meaning from the individual's frame of reference; and both require serious effort and serve as ways for students to take intellectual control. They are separated only for purposes of emphasis and instructional attention. When a middle school teacher develops student mathematical reasoning by having his students play chess, he is encouraging them to think about how many times a king is prevented from capturing a piece that has moved against him because it is protected by one or more opposing pieces (critical thinking), and he is encouraging students to imagine the relationship between the king and pawns—eight pawns dedicated to protecting the king and eight dedicated to attacking him (creative thinking).

In general, teaching thinking indirectly or directly is a part of "regular" teaching by good teachers in all school grades and disciplines. Yet neither critical nor creative thinking are being taught sufficiently. Critical thinking can be defined as reasonable reflection focused on deciding what to believe or do; it is generally used to test, refine, and evaluate assertions or ideas. Critical thinking is usually taught by teachers in conjunction with appropriate content in mathematics, science, English, and social studies and is, in fact, a fundamental part of these subjects. It is, and can be, learned by all students as they "take" the core curriculum. A popular way to teach critical thinking is through scaffolding, or erecting a structure to support student critical thinking and then dismantling the structure when the thinking is culminated or the task requiring the thinking is complete. Scaffolding is most useful when students are just learning to think critically or when they are experiencing some trouble. Examples of scaffolding are the teacher "thinking aloud" for a student, prompting a student with a checklist, asking students questions as a way of guiding them through a problem, or giving a student hints or cues as to how to proceed.

Creative thinking by way of simple definition is the ability to produce an idea, product, or way of doing something that is new, unique, original, or nonexistent before in the experience of the individual, usually in relation to fulfilling a need or solving a problem. Teaching creative thinking tends to be more of an extra accompaniment to the regular school curriculum. It doesn't get much direct or indirect emphasis or attention and gets into the classroom mostly when a few interested teachers choose to teach it, perhaps with creative writing assignments. And it doesn't matter if the creative thinking turns up what has been accomplished previously. Joyce, Weil, & Calhoun (2000), a contemporary educational writer on teaching methods, states it is necessary to reinvent the wheel every once in a while, not because we need a lot of wheels but because we need a lot of inventors! Teachers who do teach creative thinking directly (or at least nourish its growth in students through guided discovery, for example) recognize it is not a single distinctive ability nor is it just a matter of talent. Teachers who approach creative thinking only on the grand scale and believe it is the province of a few who do it "naturally" (Beethoven, Einstein) may miss opportunities to foster in all students modest creative achievement from creative thinking that can provide both academic payoffs and personal rewards.

Creative thinking is carried out in a way that may be often rather messy for both teachers and students; it is frequently not linear, for instance, and it allows for emotional components and intuition to be more important than intellectual ones. But creative thinking still shows a series of clear principles at work, not necessarily in the order that follows: recognition of a felt concern or problem and a goal, appraisal of the context in which the problem is set, acceptance of aesthetics as much as practical qualities in products, attention to process (e.g., incubation, invention) as much as results (e.g., strategy selection, solutions), dependence on mobility in gathering data as much as fluency (trying an alternate perspective or making the thinking more abstract or more concrete or more general or more specific—not just generating more ideas), working at the edge of one's competence (risk taking), choosing and applying, seeking and accepting reasonable criticism and evaluation, adopting and diffusing acceptable alternatives, and adhering to intrinsic motivation more than extrinsic motivation. Available skills that help constitute the patterns of creative thinking, illustrate the principles of dependence on mobility and the like, and make creative thinking work in classroom application include the following:

Analogy—associating familiar but possibly dissimilar or seemingly unrelated things or words (*"Peaceful terror"* describes what animal? How so?) or making comparisons or contrasts for the purpose of stimulating new ideas or broadening insight into old ones (comparing myself with a car engine, *I feel as if my thoughts are igniting*). Analogies may be stated directly (metaphors): "I am a lion about this being the correct way!" Or, they may take the form of similes, which use *like* or *as* to make the comparison: "Understanding this problem is like getting rid of a cold!"

Brainstorming—generating alternatives for thinking about a problem and its possible solution; it is a two-phase process in which the thinker first comes up rapidly and somewhat spontaneously with as many different possibilities as he or she can think of (setting a predetermined number helps), then in the second phase, the ideas are carefully looked at and evaluated for their importance and their practical value. In this phase, ideas may be discarded and priorities may be given to revised ideas in terms of their likely use for the initiating problem or concern.

Challenging assumptions—asking questions about something that is taken for granted; the questions are intended to elicit information but also to create discomfort with existing explanations or beliefs or hypotheses in order to open up thinking to different perspectives, possibilities, and ways of looking at ideas and events. As a result, students may be better able to cope with the testing events of their daily lives.

Combining—putting together two or more separate things into a

127

single thing (putting together the ideas of telephone and TV produced the video phone). Using this skill means asking, "What can I put together?" and "What is the result?" Combining makes the student think hard about the nature and purpose of what is being put together and may result in finding something new to help solve a problem.

Considering consequences—making a deliberate effort to consider what might happen as a result of creative thinking in order to help evaluate and adjust present thinking. It lets a student see, for instance, that an action he or she might be inclined to take based on present thinking may not be worthwhile in the long run even if the immediate effect or result would seem to be good. Or, an action that has seemingly favorable long-term consequences may not work out to be very sound at the moment. This skill is usually done in three arenas: considering immediate and short-term consequences (right now to about 5 years), considering medium-term consequences (5 to 25 years), and considering long-term consequences (more than 25 years). The latter two may be difficult for students tending to operate in the here and now, but they are useful in educating their thinking to plan ahead and out of the current time frame.

Dominant idea—recognizing and then breaking away from the "main road" along which thinking is moving. A dominant idea is an idea that is so dominant it makes it difficult to think of any other ideas. All thinking on the subject is captured by the one idea, and other ideas are ignored. Often the dominant idea is very obvious; sometimes it is implicit—or it may be a cluster of ideas that are all equally dominant. The important thing is to put effort into recognizing an idea that dominates a situation (a dominant idea in schools is to get students through exams successfully). Once it is recognized, it is not too difficult for teachers and students to escape from it (we might consider and evaluate the idea that schools are to give students something worthwhile to do while they grow up and learn from each other and their world; the emphasis of instruction then is on keeping students productively occupied and in contact with their communities).

Fantasizing—exploratory adventures within the mind's protective wall. Fantasizing as a skill to be taught in the context of thinking creatively is "safe" because there is little, if any, required overt behavior, and students, or teachers, do not have to accept the consequences of fantasizing. Inner thoughts can be tinkered with or changed without having to explain the change to anyone; new thoughts and ideas can be "tried out" in complete privacy and discarded with no one the wiser—or used to help solve a problem. Fantasizing frees thinking to create possibilities that never before existed as well as potentially provides deeper understandings of those that did. With proper structure, activities using fantasizing (e.g., guided daydreaming) can produce an enjoyable natural high in which the student produces clues for solving problems creatively and realistically.

Forecasting—"jumping off" from present information to make a variety of predictions about the possible causes and effects of various phenomena (e.g., students' predictions about returns from parents on a poll to be given on the school's dress code, predicting what will happen next in the novel). Forecasting might be for the next moment or for the more distant future. It can derive from cognitive thinking or imagining or a combination of both. Forecasting can motivate students to dig deeper into information and connect various pieces of previously learned data in order to see if predictions hold up. It gives students an advance look at what might happen with their current alternatives or courses of action, and it allows them to work backward from anticipated consequences to create more effective futures. A well-considered forecast should push students to move from perhaps somewhat naïve assumptions to positions that reflect more critical awareness of an issue (problem, concern, idea). Follow-through activity in forecasting is crucial. Students should be helped to critique the quality of their initial forecasts in light of additional insights gained and increasingly welcomed and made comfortable in generating new and better predictions for situations in which forecasting is an applicable skill.

Mental imagery—the forming of images in the "mind's eye" or the imagination, using all five senses as appropriate: seeing, hearing, tasting, touching, and smelling. ("I 'see' the full map I am making for a geography project before I begin it"; "I 'taste' the juice of my apple in my lunch before I eat it or trade it.") Mental imagery can be self-generated or more guided by the teacher. It often requires an incubation period and may provide illumination—or a sudden flash of insight—at unexpected times.

Random stimulation—deliberately mixing into present thinking an idea that comes from some unconnected source or stimulus (TV, scanning around the room, fantasizing). It can be any piece of information or idea; its initial relationship to what is being thought about is not important. Rather, it is used to disturb present thinking patterns and break through any blocks that might be hindering the effectiveness of thinking. Random stimulation results in a restructuring of thinking and may help produce some new ways of thinking on an initiating problem or concern.

Reversal—thinking in an opposite direction to provide a new and helpful way to consider a confronting situation or problem. Reversal begins with noting thoughts the way they are and then doing a provocative rearrangement of them to see what develops. Any form of reversing will suffice: Arrange ideas from back to front or from inside out (i.e., think from "inside" a problem); or think backward from a desirable conclusion; or think inductively, going from specific examples to a main concept or generalization. The task with reversal is to not be concerned with the "right order," or with getting an immediate answer, but to notice what happens when thoughts are turned around and how this may provide a new and helpful way to consider information, which, in turn, could lead to the solution of a problem.

Suspending judgment—delaying judgment in order to help an idea survive longer, breed further ideas and perspectives of the individual thinker, permit collection of additional data, encourage forthcoming ideas of others, allow backing away from the problem or situation to permit time to play upon its complexities, and permit ideas that seem "wrong" within the current frame of reference to last long enough to show that the frame of reference or problem needs altering or redefining. Even suspending judgment on what students *know* is true can often lead to answers that are equally, albeit differently, true.

In sum, when a teacher learns (more) about and teaches (consistently) these composite skills and creative thinking and thinking in general, he or she further develops as *a reflective practitioner who continually evaluates the effects of his/her choices and actions on others (students, parents, and other professionals in the learning community) and who actively seeks out opportunities to grow professionally* (INTASC principle 9). In parallel with the purposes of creative thinking, this INTASC principle reminds educators that teaching creative thinking produces a worthy product or outcome—helping a teacher become a true reflective (but not always popular) practitioner, and it implies a challenge. Philosopher and educator John Dewey points out that challenge when he says that thinking critically and creatively would "not involve a superficial adaptation of the existing system but a radical change in foundation and aim: a revolution (Westbrook, 1991, p. 173)."

Work Options

Small Group Discussions

Use small group discussions (five to seven students) to encourage student ownership of curricula and empower students with choices that can affect the how, what, when, and where of classroom learning. When students are motivated into becoming active stakeholders in the learning process, they learn problem-solving and decision-making skills, develop strategic and creative thinking skills, become accountable for their own performance, and are likely to be more academically challenged. Students need opportunities to negotiate how texts are understood, foresee what directions their discussions may take, and recognize how structured or fluid their conversations are. Small group discussions give the students a collaborative setting to analyze multiple interpretations of a text, to momentarily stop performing solely for the teacher, to engage in cognitive battling with self and peers, and to voice and analyze the multiple perspectives represented by their classmates. Transferring power to the students in terms of interpreting the text leads to a more dynamic interaction with the text and provides an opportunity for the students to discover and explore textual material while moving away from structures that require convergent thinking, "best" interpretations, or definitive resolutions. Students during small group discussions should be encouraged to voice their "voices" and appreciate "voices" that sound different.

Creative Conversations for Helping Students Examine Their World

Engage students in conversations that help them creatively (and critically) examine their world. Create a classroom culture that promotes questioning. Ask "what if" questions. Invite students to probe academic subject matter. Further student understanding in the classroom of how they and other students respond to characters, situations, and events in reading selections: Do they question stereotypes? Do the illustrations in a story signify oversimplified generalizations about a specific race, group, or sex? Are gender demarcations projected in leadership male roles and passive women characters? Do characters from a minority group show extraordinary qualities to succeed? Does the vocabulary carry sexist or exclusionary or degrading overtones to specific races or cultures or groups of people? What is the author's perspective? Ask students to maintain and share a point-of-view journal to explore the "I–it" relationship between themselves and a curriculum topic of significance.

Creative Projects

To help students develop their own creative thinking abilities, create lesson plans that challenge assumptions. Form groups of four or five students and give them discipline-related "accepted facts" that could benefit from inquiry, creative, analytic, or investigative skills. This work can help students identify distinct creative approaches used by themselves and others (e.g., use of random stimulation) and the characteristic mix of strengths and skills required to investigate effectively. Have students select a newspaper headline and create an original story. Have students select one type of graph (bar graphs, line graphs, circle graphs, pie charts) from a page in the business section of the newspaper, and ask them to chart the "hills" and "valleys" in the life of the business. Ask students to create a bar graph to chart the time devoted to commercials on each of their favorite TV shows. Let them create a pie bar to chart the percentage of time utilized for different product categories. Students can formulate their own questions in response to their findings. Have students observe license plates of cars for a week. Ask them to create a three-column log to record the numbers, write down the special phrases and words, and create thought-blurbs on the concept behind the special phrases and words. Ask students to publish their own textbooks for some part of their favorite content area. They can delete or add information, give more examples, and present the information in a different genre. For example, students could change a piece of history into a comic strip, a biographical sketch into a personal narrative, math word problems into different forms of poetry, and so on. Ask students to publish web pages about teen issues of fitting in, academic short- and long-term goals, relationships, and identity.

Creative/Critical Connections and Media

Stimulate the creative and critical thinking of students by integrating study of media into the curriculum through articles, handouts, TV clips, and other media. To trigger discussions, ask students questions such as the following: What role do media play in our shifting perceptions? Whose perspective do we get in the news, and why does it matter? What is the importance of "missing voices" in media? What propaganda techniques influence *your* decision-making faculty? Is "telling it all" important in media messages? What is the purpose of exaggeration, satire, humor, irony, ridicule, and loaded words in media? Who controls media? Can media be controlled? What criteria do you think should be used when assessing the independence, fairness, and accuracy of a story? Are there principles that govern what and how the media report the news? If so, what do you think they are? Do you think your favorite news media source is independent, fair, and accurate? Why or why not? In addition to critical discussions, students can strengthen their creative thinking by considering how media influences decision making by evaluating the strategies used by the media to persuade readers. Students form small groups of four or five to identify the USP (unique selling point) for advertisements in a TV commercial and present them on a poster board answering the following questions: What is the purpose of the message? What techniques are being used (loaded words, bandwagon, testimonial, mudslinging, faulty cause and effect, transfer)? What meaning might the message have for different people? What point of view is represented, and what information or points of view are missing? Students can evaluate and rate the advertisements based on a rubric created by the whole class. For an extension activity, students could create their own commercial based on techniques learned from their prior analysis and study. As a follow-up activity, students can visit www.un.org/cyberschoolbus/gallery/peace/index.asp to view a picture gallery of a peace exhibit created by children from around the world and select one picture to create a peace ad based on one or more of the advertising techniques.

Creative Movements

Integrate creative physical activities such as painting, dancing, singing, role-playing, meditation, and marching into lesson planning. Let students march, stamp, clap, and dance to different patterns and rhythms of words. This helps them break language into the elements of rhythm, pattern, and repetition. Play games with verbal cues that establish a connection between words and actions. Let students employ creative movements to express the theme of a story. Ask students to finger paint letters, create letters out of sandpaper, and use Post-it notes and markers to highlight key points and jot down their reflections. These activities encourage creative experimentation, challenge tactile senses, and enhance creative flexibility. Incorporate art into everyday lesson planning. Ask students to create a diorama in response to a story element (some students can depict the setting, some may create an important event that culminated in the climax, some may create the turning point in the story, some may use cutouts and clay sculptures to illustrate an alternate ending to the story). Students can create a sequence mural for math word problems or a timeline mural of an historical event. In addition, students can create a symbol wall or a mnemonic cue board to symbolize story themes, vocabulary words, or math formulas. To help students who struggle with math word problems, turn the process of problem solving into a story writing activity. Ask them to create their own word problems in a story format by responding to math equation titles. Students can view works of art, select two characters, and write a dialogue between them, or they can reproduce a work of art in a line form with descriptive phrases that explain the line contours.

Thinking About Thinking

Give students opportunities and guidance in thinking about their own thinking so they become more conscious of their own mental processes. This activity of "metacognition" helps students become alert to how they learn and understand how they go about the process of knowing/thinking. Through metacognition, students improve their ability to monitor their own thinking, to be conscious of their own steps and strategies during the act of problem solving, and to reflect and evaluate the productivity of their own thinking during and after the thinking act. Thinking becomes the subject matter of thinking; to think, one must think about something; moreover, thinking about thinking can improve thinking. It helps, for example, to identify for ourselves how we usually proceed with thinking ("I like to observe before getting into the thinking process"; "I need a warm-up period: For example, how many ways could I use a paper clip?") as well as how we contemplate what we know and what we don't know when we engage in the problem-solving process that accompanies thinking. One device for metacognition is to have volunteer students verbalize the stages they are going through and the strategies they use as they plan strategy and work to solve a problem; these could be tape recorded and should be discussed to bring insight to the thinker and the rest of the class (e.g., "I like to plan in advance"; "I talk to myself about the first action I should take when solving a problem"; "I'm going to organize now by listing" [inner awareness]; "When I lose concentration in reading, I return to the last thought I remember and read on with connectedness" [recovery strategy]). Another device is to ask students to generate study questions for themselves prior to and during their reading of textual material. This encourages students to think about their comprehension as well as their procedure for learning. The teacher may want to add his or her own questions or comments to enhance metacognition: "Ricardo, how did you arrive at that procedure/answer?"; "Let's work with David's strategy for a moment"; "Could we agree to label that step as an experiment in Kari's thinking?"; "Tell us where you are now in your group's problem-solving sequence and how you got there." Overall, metacognition is an indicator of the educated intellect: critical and creative.

Teaching Creative Thinking Skills Through Literature

Find pieces of frequently used literature (e.g., in classroom anthologies and school libraries) and incorporate these into your teaching of creative thinking skills. Some examples include "maggie & milly & molly & may" (ee cummings)—fantasizing, imagining; "The Secret Life of Walter Mitty" (James Thurber)—imagining; *The Most Dangerous Game* (Richard Connell)—considering consequences; "The Lady or The Tiger" (Frank Stockton)—forecasting, predicting; "The Ransom of Red Chief" (O. Henry)—reversal; "The Tell-Tale Heart" (Edgar Allan Poe)—predicting; "Rain, Rain, Go Away" (Isaac Asimov)—forecasting, predicting; "Ta-Na-E-Ka" (Mary Whitebird)—brainstorming; "A Man Who Had No Eyes" (MacKinlay Kantor)—challenging assumptions; *Let Me Hear You Whisper* (Paul Zindel)—challenging assumptions; and "Ordeal in the Owyhee Country" (Margaret Truman)—brainstorming, generating alternatives.

Guide and Follow-Up Questions for Teachers and Students

1. Do I take advantage of multimedia resources to help me teach creative thinking? A good example is the free *The Idea Book for Educators*, which tunes teachers and students in to what's happening on the History Channel and provides guides for helping students develop their thinking abilities. It's available by going online at HistoryChannel.com/classroom or AandE-.com/class. Am I aware of books in my teaching field or grade that will help me foster creative thinking by teaching creatively, books such as *A Passion for the Past: Creative Teaching of U.S. History* by James A. Percoco (1998) for grades six to

eight? One for all grades and core disciplines is *Up and Out: Using Creative and Critical Thinking Skills to Enhance Learning* by Andrew P. Johnson (2000). Am I aware of materials such as Kidspiration, a visual learning tool to help K–3 students build strong thinking skills, available from Inspiration Software, Inc., at www.inspiration.com/k8. For other materials for specific grades or subjects, request catalogs from Dale Seymour Publications, P.O. Box 10888, Palo Alto, CA, 94303; Kolbe Concepts, Inc., P.O. Box 15050, Phoenix, AZ, 85060; Good Apple, Inc., Box 299, Carthage, IL, 62321; Midwest Publications, P.O. Box 448, Pacific Grove, CA, 93950; Zephyr Press, P.O. Box 13448, Tucson, AZ, 85732-3448; the IRI Group, Inc., 200 E. Wood St., Palatine, IL, 60067; and Fiskars, 7811 W. Stewart Ave., Wausau, WI, 54401. A good overall resource is the National Center for Teaching Thinking at www.nctt.net. The center provides lesson-design handbooks containing an instructional framework, sample lessons, lesson ideas, and lesson-design tools (e.g., graphic organizers and question strategy "maps" for teaching specific thinking skills) to infuse critical and creative thinking into content instruction. Also, contact the Association for Supervision and Curriculum Development (ASCD) at 225 N. Washington St., Alexandria, VA, 22314 (703-549-9110) for their *Resources* catalog.

2. Do I use (creative) procedures for getting feedback on my teaching of creative thinking? So-called 360-degree feedback is a good example. This is a multirater/multisource process that allows educators to gather data about their teaching from multiple sources in their circles of influence. The fundamental premise is that data gathered from multiple sources are more comprehensive and objective than data gathered from only one source (e.g., the principal). Sources may be supervisors, peers, subordinates, parents, community members, students, friends, or acquaintances. The person being rated also rates himself or herself, providing important data that should not be overlooked. The role of 360-degree feedback is to allow teachers to compare their own views with the views that others have of their work. This comparison has the potential for leading

them to rethink their behavior and its impact on others. Most 360-degree feedback instruments come in the form of surveys or questionnaires. Coaching is often part of the process. The coach, invited and informed by the participant in the process, takes on the role of helping the participant reflect deeply about the findings and develop specific action plans to address professional growth needs that emerge from the findings.

3. Have I recently improved my strategies for teaching creative thinking? For instance, have I looked into Brain Gym, which is a series of simple movements done in class that enhance a student's experience of whole-brain learning? A primary source on this is *Brain Gym* by Paul E. Dennison and Gail E. Dennison (1994). Do I subscribe, if teaching in elementary grades, to Macmillan's *Creative Classroom*?

4. As a teacher, do I recognize the creative individuality of my students, and do I do some planning with fairly loose structure so as to "stretch" students while also encouraging, accommodating, validating, and valuing individual creative differences? To reach out to the wide range of creativity in my students, do I consistently teach to as many student intelligences as possible (e.g., intrapersonal, visual/spatial, interpersonal, linguistic) and differentiate instruction to include allowing some students to work independently? *And*, do I show patience and compassion for the conformist who "at this point" does not wish to pursue creativity, as well as set control points so creative action does not go out of bounds? Do I have students share their individual and group creative products with others on an ongoing basis, and do I accept a wide variety of responses to instructional activities?

5. Do my students discuss questions without getting into a verbal combative situation? When other students make constructive or creative suggestions and criticisms, are they accepted in a positive way, including by me? Do my students have original ideas to contribute to a discussion? Do I accept some attitudes and concepts for democratic living in the classroom that may be nonconventional? Do I frequently give an opportunity to my students to voice their creative views on controversial

issues? Do I conduct discussions that prompt open-ended questioning: "What do we know?" "How do we know?" "Why does it matter?" Can my students work effectively in a group; express themselves creatively in a group and be rewarded for it; show consideration for the positions and feelings of others; invent, if needed, ways to mediate conflict between group members (who or what is causing our problems; who is affected; what can we do differently to continue on?); and have plenty of opportunities to express themselves as creative thinkers?

6. Am I ready to ease up on any need I may have to hold center stage in the classroom and allow my students to increasingly take charge of their own learning and embrace and expand their own set of creative thinking skills? Have I been able to build a relaxed environment that promotes negotiations and collaboration as well as the creative thinking that comes from and leads to these two basic attributes of the creative process? Have I been able to trigger the process of creative thinking in students by giving them space for errors and false starts, leaving blanks for them to fill in, encouraging them in traveling through the curriculum in their own ways (within reason), not judging them always against a set standard, and assisting them in advancing their sense of curiosity and gaining an attitude of inquisitiveness while exploring their own creative outlets and the requirements imposed upon them? When a student asks a question, do I frequently respond as a facilitator of creative thinking by asking, "How do you think you should do it?" (and then be sure the student does process information)? Do I show respect, as deserved, for the views and decisions of students?

7. Am I aware of various programs I could use for teaching thinking? Some include *Structure of Intellect (SOI)*, available from SOI Institute, Box D, Vida, OR, 97488; *Instructional Enrichment*, available from Curriculum Development Associates, Inc., Suite 414, 1211 Connecticut Ave. NW, Washington, DC, 20036; *Strategic Reasoning*, available from Innovative Sciences, Inc., Park Square Station, P.O. Box 15129, Stamford, CT, 06901-0129; *Cognitive Research Trust (CoRT)*,

available from Pergamon Press, Inc., Fairview Park, Elmsford, NY, 10523; *Odyssey*, available from Mastery Education Corporation, 85 Main Street, Watertown, MA, 02172; *Creative Problem Solving (CPS)*, available from Creative Education Foundation, 437 Franklin St., Buffalo, NY, 14202; and *Higher-Order Thinking Skills (HOTS): A Computer-Based Approach*, available from Stanley Pogrow, College of Education, University of Arizona, Tucson, AZ, 85721

8. Do I continue to grow as a creative teacher teaching creative thinking? Do I, myself, model creative thinking with increasing frequency, such as responding to student questions in a thoughtful but "new" way? Do I maintain a creative spirit, showing, for instance, that I have fun solving problems? Do I plan activities unfamiliar to the students, intervening before students become frustrated to the point where learning ends? Do I make increasing use of higher-order questions (from me and the students) and give students sufficient time (more than the all too common one second pause) to consider them and their (creative/critical) responses to them? Do I ask students to continually reflect on what they are learning and possibly produce more effective and efficient answers and ways of operating? Do I make students conscious of their own thinking processes (point out to the class specific skills and processes used) and have them share their findings when appropriate—with me or appropriate others asking for identification, evidence, elaboration, and clarification? Do I keep significant others aware of what I am doing in my classroom (e.g., parents) and encourage their (creative) contributions? Do I at least sometimes read basic background textbooks on teaching thinking, books such as *Practical Strategies for the Teaching of Thinking* by Barry K. Beyer (1987), *Fundamentals of Creative Thinking* by John S. Dacey (1989), and *Creative Teachers, Creative Students* by John Baer (1997)?

TEACHING LIVING WITH SORROW AND LOSS

It might be as serious as one's parents getting a divorce or a 15-year-old friend being shot at school or as sophisticated as students losing, or never gaining—to their ultimate loss—an understanding of the necessity of rules. (This possibility is an outcome of 1960s legal activism: the student rights revolution. Students may not learn who fought in World War I, but they develop a sense of immunity from authority with precocious speed.) Sorrow and loss might be more from culture shock, such as the loss of their first language accompanying the learning of English by ESL students, or the missing of their old school in their home country. Or, it might spring from young love unreturned, such as the loss felt by not being "liked" by the boy you have a crush on. It might be a class's general sense of sorrow for a young soldier from the community who is killed in a war overseas or the premature death of a favorite teacher from inoperable brain cancer or one student's very personal sorrow about a low grade received on an important test. The point is that, in some way, all in the classroom community, including the teacher, suffer sorrow and loss at one time or another. It is a fact of school life and should be dealt with accordingly in the curriculum along with attention to the standards.

In loco parentis is an old concept that means "in place of parent." Some teachers feel they should no longer have this role; they see their job as preparing students for academic success—with the standards, for instance. But they are wrong. Teaching should not be a sterile or narrowly framed routine. It should include sensitivity and caring (but not overreacting) in regard to the personal lives students bring with them into the classroom. Attuned teachers can learn of students' sorrow and loss, even their tragedies, in a number of ways: by listening to their stories, by communicating with them and their parents, or by observing their physical or behavioral signs, such as withdrawal moves or attempts to get attention. One elementary school teacher we know has in her classroom a large hand-carved wooden pig with a cocked ear. She encourages children to "go talk to the pig"—and they do, often revealing their inner sorrow more easily than when approached directly. (She follows up by reminding students that it is very natural to have sorrow and feel loss; she invites those who spoke to the pig—"Piggy," by name—to visit with her when they are ready.)

Teachers who do deal with sorrow and loss in today's classrooms demonstrate their empathic concern. They show respect for the student and the student's feelings. They build the student's feelings of personal adequacy. They are willing to reveal some of the sorrow and loss in their own lives (the death of a spouse, for instance), but not to extremes or neurotic excess. Perhaps the major direct effort made currently by teachers in teaching living with sorrow and loss lies in individual classroom spin-offs from school or districtwide character education initiatives. Character education initiatives hold that widely shared and pivotally important core ethical values such as trustworthiness, caring, honesty, fairness, responsibility, and respect for self and others form the basis of good character, and these can be taught and they can be learned. Good character, in turn, helps students respond in a positive way to life's challenges, including those tied to sorrow and loss. One popular character education initiative is mentoring, in which selected (appropriately trained) and usually older students are matched with generally younger students (in a different grade) to learn from each other about life in and out of the classroom. The older mentor listens to his "buddy" on a regular basis (perhaps for a grading period), accepting feelings and frustrations and sharing feedback while modeling the core values of his own good character. The mentor, in the process, may well gain insights into his own situations of sorrow and loss. Overall, incorporating mentoring into instruction in its different versions, such as same-class academic mentoring, is particularly effective for teaching living with sorrow and loss to middle and high school students (e.g., what to do with sorrow over an assignment that won't be ready to meet the deadline). Many lower grade teachers like to use the character education initiative of bibliotherapy techniques—reading fiction and non-fiction books, stories, and poems that help students recognize the universality of sorrow and loss and how others cope with these twin realities.

The concept of *connections* provides at least a partial definition for teaching living with sorrow and loss. The concept associates connections with being part of the human race. We all experience sorrow and loss from our connections to others—friends, parents, and people with whom we come into contact. Students who experience sorrow and loss, for instance, may often also come to recognize self-connection to accompanying personal fears (e.g., kindergarten children may fear "losing" their families as they first begin attending school). Connections, as embraced in INTASC principle 10, involve the larger community beyond the classroom the teacher uses to effectively teach living with sorrow and loss. In this bigger picture, the teacher is required to *foster relationships with school colleagues, parents, and agencies in the larger community to support students' learning and well-being.* In sum, the multifaceted concept of connections may open up to teachers the idea of teaching living with sorrow and loss as it closes down this chapter in our book.

Work Options

Creative Outlets

Help students make a shift from the past to the present and engage in positive activities that blunt the pain associated with grief. Ask them to reflect on their current situation and deal with "crisis time" by reevaluating the present challenges associated with the adversity. Ask them to reflect on what is in their control and to let go of what is not in their control. Engage the student in a creative project that can redirect the student's mind away from the loss and the fears associated with the loss. Provide the students with opportunities to take control. Provide nonverbal outlets such as drawing, dancing, and journal writing for expressing grief. Offer art and play therapy to students. Creating a memoir for a lost family member helps heal the pain. Each student could participate in creating a memory board of a deceased loved one using photographs, memoirs, and messages. Designing a scrapbook of the person can help the student relive special moments with that person, which in turn can be recuperative in nature. Students could fill large helium balloons and write messages inside the balloons to the person they recently lost. Organize a nature walk as a part of a science project. Ask the students to volunteer for community service hours to help in a cognitive shift of the loss. With proper permissions, conduct field trips to the cemetery and a funeral home. A poetry unit on the theme of death can help students better understand their reactions when dealing with death and express pent-up emotions associated with loss.

Coping Strategies

It is important for the student to become aware of a denial mode and face the loss. Speak to the student to identify escape strategies that she might have adopted: keeping too busy, socializing too much, sleeping for too long. If you find that the student is resisting coming to terms with the loss or is experiencing guilt pangs, set up a meeting with the school counselor. It is important for students to examine their unrealistic expectations and try to get rid of guilt pangs that are connected with circumstances over which they have no control. Talk to students about their future plans and goals. This can help them put their loss in a timeline perspective and regain their faith in their future. Advise parents to send their children on a weekend camp, which provides them personal space to express and deal with their grief. Ask students to take some self-renewing alone time to read inspiring books, write poetry, listen to uplifting music, reflect on positives, write in a journal, go for a walk, play a musical instrument, or meditate. Integrate a "tune in" time within your lessons for the students to simply pause and reflect on the loss of a loved one. The theme of death can be linked with lessons in different content areas: students can create a fictional story board of an organism's life span based on scientific facts; design a poster on changing seasons to explain the cycle of life; or read stories on grief, forgiving oneself, and discovering a spiritual anchor. They can participate in small group discussions; create timelines of historical figures who survived personal tragedies; design graphs on a research study of natural calamities; write journal entries on their traumatic experiences; or create a vocabulary board with affirmative phrases such as "I can cope with this," "I will survive this," and "I can control my mind and think the thoughts I choose."

Dealing With Tragedies

The September 11, 2001, attacks brought this reality to the surface: Anyone is vulnerable to life's tragedies. A tragedy of this proportion can arouse emotions ranging from anger to bitterness to shock. Children as well as adults can exhibit trauma symptoms. Here are some of the reactions common in students: withdrawal, absenteeism, changes in academic performance, increased hyperactivity and decreased concentration, defiance, hate statements, anger outbursts, numbness, passivity, and anxiety and fear about safety of self and others. When disaster affects the whole school community, the teachers can play a critical role in the healing process. Make changes to the classroom routine. Give students time to deliberate over the event, and if necessary, hold discussions on the students' fears and concerns. Listen carefully and respect a student's wish not to talk. Express your own emotions and share the I-messages that are linked to the event. It is important to let the students know it is perfectly normal for an adult to share: "I feel depressed because of the crash" (or "sad"). Reassure the students of their safety, and try to determine if they are hearing words they don't know the meaning of. Prompt children to think of the positives that came out of the tragedy. Research the following websites for help:

www.cloudnet.com/~edrbsass/edsoc.htm#currentevents has lesson plans on the September 11 tragedy for middle and high school grades. The focus is on teaching tolerance, using creative detours to come to terms with September 11, and analyzing the shadow-ripples of the September 11 tragedy.

www.lessonplanspage.com/Terrorism.htm features lesson plans for K–12 and gives practical tips on dealing with terrorism in the class.

www.nytimes.com/learning/general/specials/terrorism offers interdisciplinary lessons for grades 6 to 12 based on *New York Times* articles developed in partnership with the Bank Street College of Education in New York City.

www.esrnational.org/antidiscriminationlesson.htm provides useful lessons on stereotypes, prejudice, and discrimination for grades 6 to 12.

Establishing Positive Connections

Help students seek positive connections within their school community and create a circle of positive people around them who can help them with the change. Encourage peer counseling and mentoring. Maintain a loss inventory to identify bereaved students, and schedule grief groups so they can share their loss and grief. Conduct discussions that prompt meditative introspection. Design lesson plans on the inevitability of the event and the inevitability of this moment passing. Conduct structured discussions on the students' philosophy of death. Share stories that prompt existential questions concerning life and death. Questioning can help get the bitter edge out of the loss. The class sits in a circle and explores issues of body, mind, spirit, and relationships. Students engage in reflective discussions on real-life issues and ask open-ended questions: Have you experienced guilt for something you had no control over? Is death a cessation of body, mind, and spirit? Is it normal to brood over the memories associated with dead people? Talking about grief can help bridge the awkward zone of loss and can provide students with new insights and practical strategies to deal with grief. Conduct an in-circle and out-circle activity on emotions associated with loss—have students in the in-circle move to the music and find a person from the out-circle when the music stops. Ask the in-circle students to share their experience with the death of a loved one, elaborating on the feelings they experienced and a coping strategy that helped them heal. Students can learn from their peers and teach their peers strategies to deal with fears related to a tragic event.

Routines

Establish fairly predictable, but not rigid, classroom routines. These should be routines with which students are not necessarily totally comfortable, but ones which they believe can help them develop the strength to do the risk taking that often involves some fear as well as sorrow and loss. A routine continually fosters in a variety of ways the attitude that grading is corrective feedback, not a "death sentence" for those who suffer, say, the loss of an expected high grade and hold a binding degree of sorrow over what that might do to their academic records.

Developing Emotional Intelligence

From sources such as *Emotional Intelligence: Why It Can Matter More Than IQ* (1995) and *Educating for Character: How Our Schools Can Teach*

Respect and Responsibility (1991), plan lessons that teach students how to recognize and manage their emotions. Include a lesson on the need to develop the strength of character and the compassion accompanying emotional maturity that allows for realistically accepting sorrow and loss.

Room and Personal Decorations

Decorate your classroom with the help of students. With colored construction paper, plants, large panels documenting students' ideas and the like, make it a cheerful environment in which to "live" and work. Wear clothes yourself that are "sharp," attractive, and professional and that do not lend themselves to an atmosphere of doom and gloom.

Providing Play Time

Give young students class time for dramatic or constructive play to allow them to suspend reality in order to create outcomes in which they can feel some comfort as they come to grips with the sorrow and loss in their lives (e.g., make something to commemorate loss, such as a mural). Be sure to provide some overall supervision. It helps to have safe props, blocks, and so on in the play areas. It is also important to develop a system through which students can talk to an adult when and if that kind of interaction is appropriate (a parent volunteer or teacher aide or "talk table" would work). A well-trained and cared for "listening" dog works very well—if the animal can be brought into the classroom.

Mini-Lessons in Learning to Deal With Sorrow and Loss

Reassure students, through discussion, that it is natural to feel sad; it is part of the life cycle. Allow students to use art or produce puppet scenarios for private expression of their grief. "Return" the student from his significant sorrow back into the class by assigning him a special task, such as choosing a group activity or feeding the fish.

Invite students to create and send letters to someone they know who is sick or sad—perhaps in a situation similar to theirs. This helps develop empathy for others at a time of sorrow and loss and perhaps helps with one's own sorrow. Encourage pretend activity for development of emotional skills (e.g., role-play interacting with a peer whose pet has died). This can help develop skills for dealing with ones' own sense of loss.

Recognizing Commonalities

Invite students to list ways in which all people are alike: for instance, all human cultures have family units, power relationships, divisions between male and female roles, religious beliefs, evidence of social status, celebrations of some sort, a useable language system, tool development and use, cooperative arrangements, stylized movements such as ritual dance, explanations as to how nature works and why things happen as they do (scientific theory, myth), a need for love and to express love, and the instinctive responses of sucking, crying, smiling, attempting to be mobile (walking), and exploring. Discuss with students why *ways to express felt sorrow and loss* should be added, if it is not already on their list. Support students in portraying sorrow and loss in either an objective fashion (giving a current newspaper report detailing a public sorrow from the lack of a cure for cancer) or a subjective/personal one (writing a poem about a personal loss) as a normal part of being human.

Guide and Follow-Up Questions for Teachers and Students

1. Do I understand that there is not one standard pattern of reaction to traumatic experiences and that it is a highly idiosyncratic activity? Preschoolers might associate death with a fairy-tale magical event that can be made reversible; elementary school children may objectively distance themselves from a loss situation and might experience difficulty understanding the implications of death; middle school children may express their grief by going on a self-destructive spree; high school students may simply withdraw and want to brood in their cocoons. As a teacher, am I sensitive to the reactions of my students, which can range from regressive behaviors to explosive behaviors to passive behaviors?

2. As a teacher am I aware that children, unlike adults, often take a longer time to overcome grief? With their lack of questions

or their tendency to keep to themselves, it might appear to adults that they have come to terms with the situation, but internally they may be experiencing confusion or complex emotions they feel reluctant to share.

3. Do I listen to my students? Listening to them is critical in moving away from stereotyping their behaviors during their crisis time. Do I bond with them and empathize with them? Am I reaching out to my students, acknowledging their pain, and getting them to talk about their grief? Am I listening to denial and masking cues in students? Some students deny their grief and engross themselves in temporary distractions, which in turn postpone the healing process.

4. As a teacher am I willing to improve my understanding of my students' mode of thinking when dealing with death, depression, and suicide? To get a better understanding of students' idiosyncratic reactions toward loss, it might help me to read these books: *On Death and Dying* by Elisabeth Kubler Ross (1997), *The Last Dance* by Lynne and Strickland DeSpelder (2004), and *Depression and Suicide in Children and Adolescents* by Philip G. Patros and Tonia Shamoo (1988).

5. Am I aware of what school and community resources are available for grieving students? For example, there is a grief training program called *Kids Grieve Too* for teachers, administrators, and school counselors. (Developed by Hospice of Washington DC, the program offers help to teachers to address grief-related problems, make appropriate referrals, and initiate classroom intervention.) Specifically, am I well connected to the guidance counselors and crisis teams and other support personnel within *my* school to help with sorrow and loss experienced by my students?

6. Do I provide opportunities for students to identify and share their own varied personal abilities and talents? Do I give public recognition to these? (Students who are proud of their own strengths will be more likely able to deal effectively with sorrow and loss and can be seen, if public mention is made of these strengths, as resources by other students.)

7. Does my instruction include tools that might give me some

clues as to current feelings of sorrow and loss in my students? For example, I could have younger students draw a face (happy/sad) that best illustrates their feelings about a particular situation (e.g., the accomplishment or lack thereof of their task-oriented group). I could ask students to complete some relevant sentence stems: "When I need to add fractions in this class, I _____" (feel strongly my loss of last year's fundamental math skills). For a good source of tools for measuring empathy, get the most recent edition of *Human Relations Development: A Manual for Educators* (George M. Gazda, Frank S. Asbury, Fred J. Balzer, William C. Childers, and Rosemary E. Phelps).

IDEA SIXTEEN
TEACHING *DISRESPECT*

Students need to be able to separate the wheat from the chaff. For their own emotional and economic survival and continuing intellectual and social/psychological growth, they need to recognize, identify, and be able to deal effectively with and speak out against situations and behaviors that require a lack of esteem and proper regard. They need to learn to *disrespect*, to avoid giving acceptance, even tolerance, where it is not warranted, something that is rarely taught in schools but when done is usually part of teaching beyond the standards. There should be no tolerance on the part of students for racist and sexist epithets passed in class or scrawled on toilet stall walls. Students need a healthy and warranted disrespect for the thinking that permits driving at high speeds with a learner's permit but without an adult in the car. There is nothing to respect in unwanted homelessness, chronic obesity, adolescent excessive thinness because of cultural pressure, unexamined prejudice, or the continual coming to terms with ignorance. There is nothing to respect in welcoming poverty or rape. Students can and should learn to disrespect internet pornography, substance abuse, teenage suicide, stereotyping, drunken driving, unwanted pregnancy, continuing use of the "f-word" or its like, scams against the elderly (their grandparents), smoking, spreading communicable diseases, or being permanently and inclusively labeled "slow learner," "bad kid," "at risk," even "gifted and talented," with promises that they can be anything they want to be. (The former is binding, and the latter just isn't true.) Overall, there is much to disrespect in classroom and school life and in the adult world.

Teaching disrespect when it *is* taught is well started by helping students look *and* see. A good example involves something most students are familiar with—a deck of common playing cards. Three of the kings show their full faces; the other shows a profile. In contrast to their all having *looked* at cards, almost all students will not have *seen* them enough to point out which king shows only his profile (king of diamonds; incidentally the king of diamonds represents Julius Caesar). The point is that personal growth requires both looking and seeing, and in being helped to see more fully, students increasingly recognize there is a duality to life that provides evil as well as good, things to disrespect as well as things to respect.

When teachers are more specifically guiding students to appropriately disrespect, they often focus on five lessons. The first is learning to concentrate on items for disrespect over which they have some control, unlike cancer striking their friends, or a parent's infidelity, or financial disaster. There is only a limited amount of academic learning time available in school, and it is often beneficial for students to exert energy where they can possibly make a difference. The second is to learn to monitor passion with objectivity. You want students to be passionate against intimidation, for example, but they need to stay controlled so they can most effectively apply action to change for the better what they disrespect. Not all things can be changed. The third lesson in teaching disrespect is to help students withhold judgment (e.g., not to judge too quickly that an act is bigoted and worthy of disrespect). Encouraging students to reflect and providing them time to reflect, including time to interact with others to get *their* thinking, is an important component of teaching students to disrespect. Sometimes the withholding of judgment must be speeded up to deal with the current situation. The fourth lesson is learning to recast the item for disrespect as part of the process of applying any *lasting* disrespect. For instance, the middle school student could think of her harassment by her male classmate as coming from *his* insecurity around girls—and this can change over time and with nonthreatening contacts. And the fifth lesson is helping students develop support systems where they can "check out" what they think deserves disrespect. Clearly, parents and teachers can identify themselves as available support sources and can act accordingly.

In sum, teaching students to disrespect, as a part of teaching beyond the standards, is legitimate but tricky and requires very careful instruction. Still, teaching students to be comfortable with giving deserved disrespect is a sensible strategy when a teacher *understands how children learn and develop and can provide learning opportunities that support their intellectual, social, and personal development* (INTASC principle 2).

Work Options

Personal Intolerance

Ask students to make a written list of things in their lives or the lives of their friends that they feel are deserving of disrespect: being called a troublemaker, hearing a car horn blown from behind while waiting on a red light before turning left, being harassed, finding deliberate placement of a virus that impacts personal electronic communication, or being treated as "slow" because of the disorder of dyslexia. Interact on these issues in class with students, or have students do presentations on them with overhead transparencies or poster board illustrations. Discuss that disrespect may not always be a continuing appropriate response (e.g., attention-deficit/hyperactivity disorder—ADHD—as a label on a student may help parents, teachers, and the student locate useful resources for advancing the student's learning at a certain point in time).

Outside Sources

Encourage yourself and your students to read newspapers and magazines (e.g., *People*) and search the Internet to locate material worthy of disrespect, and bring this material into a class discussion on why it may truly deserve disrespect. You might want to draw on the Christian Bible, where evil does exist in the form of the Devil. What kind of evil, temptations, and behaviors are found in the Bible to disrespect? What, if anything, could or should be done about these? In more contemporary times, some characters and acts in the Harry Potter books like *Harry Potter and the Order of the Phoenix* by J. K. Rowling work well as sources of material for disrespect.

Finding Examples to Disrespect

Teach students simple research skills for locating material of interest to them to disrespect. Ask students to report on where they found their material and why they chose what they did, how it relates to disrespect, and their opinion on whether it should continue to be disrespected—and why or why not. Here is a sample from sports at the higher learning level, as reported by the Associated Press in the *Washington Post* on March 4, 2004: The University of Georgia men's basketball assistant coach gave a final exam to his students in his fall, 2001, course in "Coaching Principles and Strategies of Basketball." The 20-question exam included the following:

1. How many goals are on a basketball court? A. 1 B. 2 C. 3 D. 4
2. How many points does a 3-point field goal account for in a basketball game? A. 1 B. 2 C. 3 D. 4
3. Diagram the half-court line.
4. How many fouls is a player allowed to have in one basketball game before fouling out in that game? A. 3 B. 5 C. 7 D. 0

There is plenty to disrespect here: the philosophy of the coach and his lack of respect for his students; the culture that allows this kind of exam to be accepted procedure (at least temporarily; the coach was fired); the lack of complaint by the test-taking students, who were conceivably being cheated out of at least part of a quality higher education learning experience; and the test itself (a player with five fouls may not stay on the court, so the correct answer to the fourth question—which is four fouls—was not even listed).

Saying No

Teach lessons on saying "no." Everyone has a right to say no. Students need to understand that it is okay to say no, whether to unwanted sexual relations or to getting drunk or to doing drugs or to more simple requests in everyday home or classroom life ("Let's surf the net instead of studying for the math test"). Teacher-generated examples from experience in working with students are a good way of helping students learn to say no and resist peer pressure. Also, examples supporting the value of saying no can be drawn fairly conveniently out of stories in literature (e.g., Grimm's fairy tales). A book with excellent and practical ways of teaching no in the classroom is *The Skillful Teacher* by Jon Saphier and Robert Gower (1987).

Evaluating Disrespect

Engage the students in classroom role-plays. This refers to students assuming an identity other than their own, one usually decided upon in advance. It is done to explore the essence of an event, idea, situation, problem, or (personal) motivation, but without all the aspects of reality. For example, one student might act out behavior patterns he or she believes to be consistent with someone encouraging a younger person to take up drinking alcohol on the school parking lot. Other volunteer students could react with what they feel comfortable saying or doing, one at a time or as a small group of players participating in the exercise. Following the role-play, the class could discuss the offer of "a drink" and the responses to it within the context of giving deserved disrespect. Also, they could compare and contrast behaviors and actions to *respect* with behaviors and actions to *disrespect* in the playing out of the role-play—respect, for instance, for the behaviors of the student(s) who effectively dealt with the offer. A videotape of the role-play could benefit the follow-up discussion even more.

Home Connected Thoughts

Select some interested volunteer parents who understand and agree with your teaching disrespect, and identify with them some connected thoughts that can be worked with at home—and some comments and beliefs that can be brought back into classroom activities on disrespect (e.g., saying "yes" is not automatically a sign of personal weakness; disrespecting something through being tolerant of mediocrity can be carried too far and given too easily and needs to be examined and monitored by one's self and, in some cases, with the help of mature and significant others, hence the role of parents and teachers).

Guide and Follow-Up Questions for Teachers and Students

1. Is what I am disrespecting legitimately worthy of disrespect, or is it more of just a cultural difference from what I am used to and personally believe? Explain your position.
2. Will just the passage of time throw a different, perhaps even

positive, light onto the current item for disrespect? Why or why not?

3. What deserves more than disrespect (e.g., Nazi war crimes in World War II, child abuse, Middle East terrorist bombings)? Why do these deserve more than disrespect? What are appropriate alternatives to disrespect?

4. Why is it often quite hard to say "no"? Possible answers include that it conflicts with peer pressure; it is sometimes inconsistent with less assertive personalities or shy personalities; it is difficult to confront an authority figure; sometimes, at least at first, you may lose more than you gain.

5. Might it be useful to continue research on disrespect by checking into references such as ASCD's (www.ascd.org) *The Respectful School: How Educators and Students Can Conquer Hate and Harassment* by Stephen L. Wessler and William Preble (2003)? You could also research nonacademic material for comparing and contrasting behaviors and perspective related to disrespect and respect. One example is from *My Fair Lady*, where Eliza talks to Colonel Pickering: "You see, really and truly, apart from the things anyone can pick up (the dressing and the proper way of speaking, and so on), the difference between a lady and a flower girl is not how she behaves, but how she's treated. I shall always be a flower girl to Professor Higgins, because he always treats me as a flower girl, and always will; but I know I can be a lady to you, because you always treat me as a lady, and always will."

IDEA SEVENTEEN

TEACHING TECHNOLOGY USE

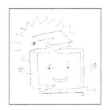

Teaching technology use, whether or not it is part of a standards curriculum, requires a skill set of how technology works and a know-how of its applications to achieve curriculum objectives; it is fundamentally associated with a "tech attitude." Tech attitude nurtures a risk-taking ability to enter a fluid and interactive world in which the teacher is willing to swap places with the students and in the process don the role of a learner. In practice, the tech attitude must include a willingness to integrate technology with ongoing instruction. When teachers actively integrate technology in the classroom, they create opportunities for the students to learn in multiple modalities and across multiple domains and enter a zone of self-directed learning. Students become exposed to a dynamic learning environment, which helps them gain an understanding that demands an active construction of meaning. Teachers, as much as students, need to take a "tech leap" and create a vibrant technology exploratory environment for their students.

When teaching technology use in the classroom, teachers are dealing with the "Nintendo generation." Students are attuned to technology and think in the hypertext. They carry their homework assignments in floppy or compact disks. Their assignment notebooks have been replaced by disks, and the no homework excuses have made a drastic transition from the dog chewing my paper or my sibling spilling milk on it to my friend pressing the delete button, or the computer crashing before the document could be printed, or the printer running out of ink. Teachers teaching technology use need to ask some serious questions about the role of technology in their classrooms. They need to find ways to get technology progressively involved in their instruction: initiate peer-to-peer communications, find a tech mentor, attend conferences, team-teach with a technology instructor, or simply experiment on a computer. They need to give up control and stop using the refrain "I will do what I know best to do." Instead they need to ask, "What are the implications of *not* integrating technology into my curriculum?"

There are three steps to teaching technology use in the curriculum: First, make sense of how technology works; second, determine how to implement it for optimum results; third, evaluate the effectiveness of the use of technology. Technology instruction should focus on the conceptual understanding of computers as well as a mastery of required skills. Deciding to teach technology use and integrate technology into curriculum is closely associated with the issue of what teachers want to teach and the impact of what is being taught. Technology can either become a mere tool for resuscitation of facts, or it can be viewed as an exciting process to augment critical thinking skills. Students working on online worksheets, typing scrolls of essays, and aimlessly browsing Internet websites tend to reveal a scenario in a classroom where teachers resist technology. Teachers need to integrate technology and its use into their larger objectives and treat technology as another tool for learning that, along with books, pencils, graph paper, construction paper, blocks, and field trips, can foster new understandings in students.

In sum, teaching technology use requires a tech attitude, risk-taking ability, a forward looking and flexible outlook (technology is constantly being updated), and careful lesson planning. By making a conscious decision to teach technology use and integrate it into his or her instruction, *the teacher understands how students differ in their approaches to learning and creates instructional opportunities that are adapted to diverse learners* (INTASC principle 3).

Work Options

Collaborative Learning Experiences

Inform students that technology facilitates collaboration and cooperation among learning. The students can construct meaning for themselves through multidisciplinary, project-based learning experiences, which encourage global collaborative interactions. Students can interact with web pals in other countries to gather information about cultural diversity. They can research the ethnic groups of that country and create a multimedia report. Multileveled online mentoring projects can involve students from different grades and different schools. Have pairs or small groups of students access a website to collect data or information that can be used by the whole class. This works especially well if the classroom is equipped with two or three computers. Students can use real-life data and graph the results using the graphing program. Students can be paired with each other to complete projects that involve community research, collection of data, graphing the results, and presenting their findings in a PowerPoint slide show. Visit www.eduplace.com/projects to browse through a list of online projects for teachers, create your own, and post it online. Students can publish their writing on the web, to be viewed, edited, and critically analyzed by a web pal.

Tech Mind-Set

Model technology use for students by using technology yourself in a variety of ways. Team-teach subject areas with a teacher from a different grade level, using the Internet to collaborate. Create a department-level website or your own web page. Post unit objectives, essential questions, assignment due dates, homework assignments, examples of students' work, lesson plans, crosscurricular integration projects, and study skill tips for students. Post the links to websites that provide homework assistance, such as www.yourhomework.com (facilitates the posting of homework assignments and provides links for students and teachers to communicate), www.homeworkhelp.com (provides links to lessons in different content areas and also to test preparation assistance), and discoveryschool-.com (offers resources and homework tips for students). Create different types of spreadsheets to keep a record of grades or student participation in class discussions. Microsoft Excel can be used for recording grades, grouping charts for small group projects or discussions, and creating a parent–teacher communication record chart. Numerical data can be graphed, sorted, and filtered using the Excel tools. The *PowerSchool PowerPack* is a web-based student information system with scheduling, grade tracking and reporting, attendance, student demographic information, and form letter generation features. Use e-mail for collaborative planning between teachers across grade levels and content areas and to communicate student progress to parents. Send classroom newsletters via e-mail to the parents of the students.

Functional Websites

With student volunteer "tech assistants" helping, make instructional use of the following websites:

- www.enc.org/topics/edtech and www.nap.edu/readingroom/ books/techgap/index.html—These websites give you a reflection platform for contemplating the role of technology in education, its relation to academic achievement, the current technological techniques and their effectiveness in a classroom, and the multiple applications of technology.
- www.ozline.com/learning/stumble.html—From this, learn the possibilities of the World Wide Web; surf selective web sources and create your own distinctive web page.
- rubistar.4teachers.org—This one helps you use customized templates to create rubrics for your project-based learning activities.
- www.handheldlearning.org—Visit this website to learn multiple uses of handheld computers or personal digital assistants (PDAs) in a classroom environment. PDAs not only drastically reduce traditional paperwork but also help students exchange team projects and information, maintain a schedule of homework assignments, create grade charts, and download notes and missed assignments. Palm handheld computers give students the mobility they need to learn and interact with information wherever they are.
- www.classroom.com—This site is useful for teachers who are always on the lookout for innovative ways to integrate technology into their classrooms. More than 30,000 teachers share their classroom experiences and expertise pertaining to integration of technology into their classrooms.

Technology Integration

Start small. Initiate the technology movement one step at a time. Don't get too ambitious in the beginning. Be realistic and start with a simple project; gradually work up to more advanced technologies. Here are some quick ways to integrate technology into lessons: Students can use the HyperStudio program to create a multimedia storyboard slideshow on a story from their literature unit. HyperStudio is a multimedia authoring system that combines text, sound, and motion into a single presentation. Students can use the KidPix program to draw freehand and manipulate clip art. Inspiration for grades 4 to 12 and Kidspiration for K–3 are programs that can work for webbing and mapping assignments. They can create a KWHL chart (what you Know, What you want to learn, How you will learn it, and what have you Learned) or a word graph (multiple definitions, parts of speech, a list of five synonyms and five antonyms, a visual signifying their meaning, or a mnemonic cue). Students can create flow charts (to describe the different classifications in life sciences) or brainstorming webs (for the prewriting stage) in the graphic programs. The students can use the highlight tool in MS Word to identify the topic sentence and clincher sentences in paragraphs and to highlight different types of speech and examples of figurative language. The Word program can give a word count and the reading level of writings. Students can construct a press release, newspaper article, news bulletin, or video news report covering current events in the setting of a novel. They can use a multimedia encyclopedia to research famous historical figures from the era being studied in a social studies unit. Students can present PowerPoint presentations for clarifying or explaining concepts, summarizing key points, highlighting thought triggers, or initiating discussions and reflections.

E-Mail Connections

Remind students that e-mail helps make instant connections across the globe. Students can post questions to people across the globe; do peer revision of writing samples; contact authors and specialists; keep an online discussion going on the books they are reading; engage in tutorial projects involving students of diverse abilities, parents, and community volunteers; or share information on classroom group projects. Establish a classroom e-mail forum where students can respond to their reading in the form of e-mail messages. Visit the Gaggle Network at www.gaggle.net to set up safe, teacher-controlled e-mail accounts for students. This is a free e-mail service for students, with good teacher controls and filters.

Making Technology Judgments and Evaluations

Make sure that students have the ability to make informed judgments about the material on the web. Teachers can compile a set of guidelines for the students to evaluate material on the Internet. It is beneficial to review guidelines with the students for computer usage. "Tech etiquette" and copyright policies should be discussed in detail, and both teachers and students should be familiar with the school system's acceptable use policy.

Post for students information on the appropriate use of the Internet and e-mail. It is also beneficial to discuss various strategies to handle potentially bad situations students might encounter while surfing the net. Ask students to create a matrix or rubric for evaluating websites. The Assessment and Rubric Information area of Kathy Schrock's website (school.discovery.com/schrockguide/assess.html) offers links to a variety of evaluation tools.

Teachers need to take a proactive approach while monitoring students during Internet use. It is strongly recommended that teachers review online material before using them with the students. Visit www.safekids.com/kidsrules.htm or www.safeteens.com to get ideas on Internet safety lessons. Providing access to more than 180,000 prescreened quality Internet resources, netTrekker is a search engine that can be trusted by teachers. To cut down on the students' try and hit method of procuring information on the Internet, teachers can use free online lesson-planning tools, such as Filamentality (www.Filamentality.com); TrackStar (trackstar.4teachers.org/trackstar/index.jsp); and S.L.A.T.E. (landmark-project.com/slate.php3).

Guide and Follow-Up Questions for Teachers and Students

1. Do I look at efficiency concerns when I teach technology use? How can I make students accountable for their behavior and learning during computer time? How can I ensure equitable use of computers within a lesson of 50 minutes? How much time should I designate to teaching computer skills and teaching content area?
2. What is my reaction when a student asks, "How do I use that program?" Do I instantly provide the answer or wait for a

response from other students before answering the specific query? Remember, students can learn complex technology applications rapidly, and peer tutoring can work well in a situation where there is a good intermix of students with different technology skills.

3. What kind of technology skills should the students practice to meet project goals? Does available software provide more advanced applications for the technologically astute students?

4. Does my school provide technical support and professional development opportunities to integrate technology into my curricula? Does the administration encourage establishing partnerships with community-based organizations such as libraries and community centers to make learning about technology and its use accessible to students *after* school?

5. Do I keep myself current on technology for use in schools? *T.H.E. Journal* is available to teachers free, and it's very informative. Go to www.thejournal.com for a subscription. (If you are especially interested in technology for math and science teaching, visit www.enc.org and ask for the free *ENC Focus Review.*)

TEACHING CONTINUING LEARNING

W hat teachers need to do as a major part of their job is to create a constant desire for continuing learning on the part of their students. We believe this should apply not just for learning in the classroom or school; or just for learning the prescribed standards, as important as they are; or just for learning during the time spent in school. The opportunity for a broad approach to continuing learning is there (we have heard the argument that between the years of 6 and 18, young people spend approximately 55% of their time in activities *other* than school and sleep!). A useful working definition of continuing learning is student-initiated study where the student proceeds on his or her own but uses informed human or material resources to help provide greater breadth and/or depth to the topic under consideration. This study is not bound by formal schooling and is maintained throughout the individual's cognitive life. It accepts that the most important resource for supporting continuing learning is ultimately the individual himself. In addition, the concept of continuing learning is one to be applied to everyone: physically handi-capped, "slow learners," "gifted and talented," "average" students, ESL students—all can and should be helped to be continuing learners regard-less of their label or reality. These categories, by the way, are *not* mutually exclusive; they often overlap. For example, a student needing a wheelchair can be gifted and talented—or not—in science. A completing thought about the definition of continuing learning is that it involves both learning for practical accomplishment in today's and tomorrow's working arenas (vocational education) as well as learning for development of the mind (academic education) so that students can continue to think critically and creatively about their life and leisure in the world around them.

Students do need help to build on their natural efforts to learn in breadth and depth about what interests them "from the cradle to the grave." They may well, however, choose not to work at continuing learning in the prescribed school curriculum. Moreover, vague willingness or good intentions to delve further into classwork ("I might check into that later") are usually not sufficient to bring about the habit of continuing learning. What does help is for teachers to assist students to identify what they might pursue (reading a biography of George C. Marshall for American history class) and to set clear goals ("I want to be able to describe the Marshall Plan from original sources"). It also helps to ensure that students are aware of the discrepancy between where they are now and their stated goals, and that they determine what the appropriate criteria are for having reached their goals. A teacher-taught process for helping students achieve goals for continuing learning is called force field analysis. In this, students are taught that their goal exists in a state of balance (equilibrium) between opposing forces: facilitating forces that exert force toward accomplishing the goal and restraining forces that hinder movement toward the desired goal (see figure 18.1).

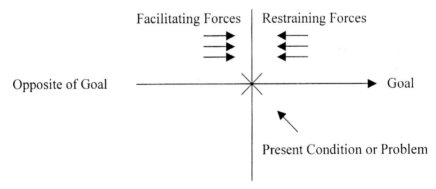

Figure 18.1 Force Field Analysis

Note: The horizontal line represents movement toward the goal. The vertical line represents problems or barriers in achieving that goal.

In doing a force field analysis, students first identify a goal for their continuing learning. They then list down the left side of a sheet of paper, or on a computer, facilitating forces that will support their reaching their goal ("I am curious about leaders in World War II"). Down the right side, they list restraining forces that are likely to block their attainment of their goal ("I tend to be lazy in going beyond what is required by teachers"). Next, students rank all their identified forces, regardless of whether they are facilitating or restraining, in terms of their influence on achieving the goal (e.g., "The force ranked number one has the most impact on my achieving my goal of all the forces I have listed"). Students then work on adding to an existing force (perhaps the one ranked number one), adding a brand new force to "overwhelm" the resistance, reducing a force, or totally eliminating a force—whatever helps them move forward toward their goal.

One popular way that teachers in schools today do advance the concept and practice of continuing learning is through the use of student portfolios. Another is through contracts and independent study projects, both with mutually understood and agreed-to objectives. Still another is self-pacing, where students who show a certain amount of self-direction are allowed to carry increasing responsibility for their work, particularly its timing, with subtle guidance from the teacher. But probably the biggest contributor in schools to facilitating continuing learning is the climate of the classroom. An inviting climate offers students a variety of opportunities to achieve success with the standard curriculum, pursue their own interests, take risks, and learn. It engages their imagination while convincing them that they are people of talent who can accomplish something worthwhile in the very difficult world in and out of the classroom. Such a climate is built on mutual respect and empathy and functions as a caring community of learners with the teacher "first among equals," who encourages students into saying, "I want to discover more about that," or "This makes me think of other things I'd like to investigate," or "With the options available, I'm excited about working with my friends as additional resources for getting the job done and seeing where our work may lead."

Classroom climate is made up of many factors (e.g., noting connections among subject areas, dealing proactively and effectively with violence, paying attention to social and ethical dimensions of learning as well as intellectual dimensions), and it is constantly changing in minor or major ways. (Greek philosopher Heraclitus once observed that you can't step in the same river twice. The water will be different; you will be different.) Nonetheless, if classroom climate is to influence continuing or lifelong learning in a positive way, its bottom line is to help students realize that they ultimately control their own pursuit of learning and that life as a self-directed learner is exciting, productive, interesting, enjoyable (with pitfalls), and well worth living.

In sum, being a continuing learner is caught up in the Smart Brief Quotes (ASCD) of politician John Foster Dulles comment "the measure of success is not whether you have a tough problem to deal with, but whether it's the same problem you had last year" and in Danish religious philosopher Soren Kierkegaard's comment "life can only be understood backwards; but it must be lived forwards." An effective classroom teacher advances the desire for problem solving and new knowledge and the practice of forward living, which are at the heart of continuing learning, when he or she *understands how children learn and develop and can provide learning opportunities that support their intellectual, social, and personal development* (INTASC principle 2).

Work Options

Personal Discovery Sheet

Invite students to fill out a personal discovery sheet on their current learning process, in which they respond to questions such as these: How satisfied are you now with your learning abilities? What are five of your strengths as a learner? What are three things you could do to strengthen yourself as a learner? What are some advantages to you in becoming a *continuing* learner? When did you last think "outside the prescribed (math, English, social studies, science) box," and what was that thinking? What happened to it? How involved are you with *this* class, and what could *you* do to become more involved? Are you a person who, overall, has a habit of thinking/planning/anticipating ahead? What are some examples of when you anticipated what you might do next in your learning? What were the results?

Independent Projects

Assign independent projects of interest to students following these guidelines: (1) The teacher agrees to the topic and method of investigation; (2) the process demonstrates students' ability to apply skills and knowledge; (3) the teacher provides guidance, structure, and mentoring as requested or necessary (e.g., sets up timelines to prevent procrastination); (4) process logs are used to document the process throughout the study; and (5) criteria for success, known to all participants, are established and agreed to at the outset—with room for modification and with attention to high standards for the product.

Portfolios

Encourage the use of portfolios. A portfolio is a collection of materials students create to document their intellectual, social, emotional, and personal development. They can vary in presentation from simple binders to digital portfolios on a CD-ROM. Portfolios may contain all kinds of conventional or less conventional self-expressions; one example is a self-portrait series: pictures a student makes of herself at various points in the academic year as the student continues to learn about her subject of interest—in this case, herself. Coaching from the teacher is a critical part of portfolio development, as is holding students to high but realistic standards while helping them realize their talents through which they can reach these standards.

Watching and Learning

Encourage students to watch educational television channels such as the History Channel or the Public Broadcasting System or A&E. (Free program guides are generally available from these resources.)

Career Preparation Experiences

Facilitate opportunities for students to engage in career preparation experiences such as spending a day with an automobile technician or a professional athlete or a fast food chef or a computer salesperson or a medical technician or a doctor or lawyer. This enables students to learn how to invent or reinvent themselves. Through flexible requirements and criteria by the teacher, the experience(s) could be connected to course credit.

Guide and Follow-Up Questions for Teachers and Students

1. Given the increasing diversity in classrooms, am I as "teacher" developing increased multicultural competencies and under-

standings about different cultures and intelligences to help make every child a continuing learner in line with his or her own background and abilities? For example, you may find your Hispanic students can pursue learning best when they have a close (professional) relationship with their teacher and when they can interact with their peers, while students from other cultures may work well on their own and not highly involve their emotions in learning academic content. (An excellent free magazine on Arab and Muslim cultures is *Saudi Aramco World*, at www.Saudiaramcoworld.com).

2. Do I encourage a multiple perspective approach to learning so that students might be more motivated to learn on their own? For example, in a unit on the Civil War, students could research and role-play slaveholders, Northern factory owners, abolitionists, or Union or Confederate soldiers and argue the respective points of view. (Students could volunteer for the role they find *least* compatible with their current views.)

3. In my classroom, are questions delivered *by students* at a variety of levels and in a mix of forms? For example, low-level, fill-in-the-blank questions ("Columbus had _____ ships?") or analysis-level discussion questions ("What alternatives to dropping the atomic bomb on Hiroshima did President Truman have?"). (Students learning to ask different level questions of one another may find they enjoy the process of probing, and that may continue over to how they deal with their own continuing learning.)

4. Do I encourage continuing learning through using a variety of teaching methods to stimulate student interest in subject matter, methods such as deductive and inductive reasoning; student hands-on exploration in contrast to full-time teacher talk; individual, pair, or trio projects as opposed to a total "assign, study, recite, test" routine and whole-class and small group discussion? Are these methods geared to enabling each student to experience feelings of competence, usefulness, curiosity, optimism, and joy in learning on a regular, if not daily, basis?

5. Is my classroom arranged, decorated, and run so that invitations to continuing learning are bountiful and students come

169

to realize that learning does not begin and end at the class-room door? (Invitations may come out of alliances with the larger community.)

6. Is there an element of "prior inventory" involved with my teaching continuing learning? For example, are students checked or do they conduct a self-inventory to see if they are computer literate? Or do they know "how to learn" at a funda-mental level (e.g., use a thesaurus, identify simple research steps and questions, use a library, interview, write with clarity and in a concise fashion)?

CONCLUSION

In this book, we've offered no silver bullet for teaching beyond the standards if that is what you choose to do. It is definitely one way to adhere to the No Child Left Behind Act. We have argued that those teachers who truly care for this nation's students *should* extend student knowledge beyond the standards, and we have offered 18 reasonable and interrelated extensions (our *ideas*), with work options for carrying them out in the classroom. Certainly, we hope you share our belief in the importance of teaching beyond the standards—in essence, to educate the whole child—and we definitely invite you to adapt and adopt our ideas and options as a starting place. You will need to add more of your own thinking as you work with your unique students.

The whole process of teaching beyond the standards is sort of like eating an elephant. You start biting somewhere (we've given you 18 suggestions). It doesn't matter that much where you start (begin with our idea 18, if you wish). After you have eaten a lot, most of the elephant (teaching beyond the standards) still remains. Remember, we advocate teaching the standards for all kinds of reasons, including that of letting those who pay for schools make sure they are getting value for their money and because professional teachers do the job they are assigned to do and do it well, as evidenced at least in part by the generally good results attained by their students in high-stakes testing on the standards. We also have no problem with teaching to the test. That seems like a smart idea to us, teaching students to know how to take tests and to know specific sets of facts. But we contend that teaching to the test is insufficient in developing well-rounded intellects and people.

We are not worried that teaching beyond the standards will require any extensive and controversial transforming of the school or classroom culture, "the way we do things around here." We believe teaching the prescribed curriculum, the standards, or even the traditional curriculum, can go hand in hand with teaching our recommended 18 ideas. (True, you

171

may have to be somewhat of a competent juggler.) And we also are convinced most teachers *want* to be the best they can be in helping students thrive (be resilient) despite set-backs (low test scores) and come eventually into more complete possession of their full powers. That means to us definitely teaching beyond the standards. It means including in the curriculum teaching that enables students to become mature, socially competent, self-disciplined, physically and mentally fit learners, creative thinkers, and problem solvers. It means helping students gain a realistic, positive self-concept and be effective and efficient communicators and listeners, as well as continuing learners who enjoy the discipline of intellectual effort both in and out of the classroom. It means taking seriously *all* of our 18 ideas and teaching them, perhaps as we have suggested, one every two weeks throughout the regular school year.

Now that you have reviewed our ideas, work options, and follow-up questions for teachers and students, all keyed to reflective thinking and presented in an informal writing style, we recommend you develop your own reflective culture of inquiry to go with them. This is done not by being an isolated teacher living behind your classroom door, but by being one who actively interacts with and asks questions of self, students, colleagues, and significant others (e.g., parents): "How can time be made to teach both the standards and beyond the standards?" (The 75,600 minutes in the typical school year allows the well-organized teacher to do both.) "Are my students learning what I value for them to learn (e.g., manners, charm), and how well?" "Are we, teacher and students, enjoying as well as learning what we are doing in the classroom?" "What resources could we use to bolster our work, and where can we get these resources (e.g., check online: shop.ascd.org)?" "If we, as teachers, observed one another teach, what might we learn to help our own teaching of the standards and beyond?" In addition to the use of inquiry, you might want to set up action research groups (of students and/or teachers) and conduct one-to-one conferences to gain information on the implementation and successes of teaching beyond the standards.

It is also important to ask questions of yourself as a teacher: "What should I be doing differently to really embrace teaching beyond the standards?" "How would my teaching be improved if I worked with the 18 ideas?" "Do I have, or am I willing and able to gain, the knowledge and skill to link what I have to teach and what I want to teach to what matters to my students?" "Will I feel a healthy personal and professional challenge in mobilizing myself and my resources to, perhaps, take a risk and teach beyond the standards?" However you go about teaching beyond the standards, using your own background and thinking and perhaps our book, we ask you to continue to develop your critical adult mind while maintaining a childlike sense of wonder and appreciation for the knowledge you now have and can employ and for the learning experiences and mentoring people you will encounter on your journey and have already encountered. Noted educator Ron Edmonds reminds us, "We can, whenever and wherever we choose, successfully teach all children whose schooling is of interest to us. We already know more than we need to know in order to do that" (1979, p. 23).

So, we conclude our book targeted to helping you learn and teach beyond the standards while leaving you with the ongoing instructional opportunities presented by the INTASC (1992) principles, which are incorporated into our text and which make teaching beyond the standards perhaps a bit more "legitimate" for conservative teachers. These 10 principles (see Appendix B) shift teaching from the perception that it is simply disseminating information to the recognition that teaching is developing learners. *Teaching Beyond the Standards*, with all of its components, develops learners, and we joyfully invite you into the action.

TWO SAMPLE LESSON PLANS

Direct Teaching of Idea 1: Teaching Awareness and Organization

Lesson Title: Measuring Personal Temperature
Third Grade: Mathematics
Estimated Time Frame: 50 minutes start-up with continuing time as needed
Students: 18
Essential Questions:

Does everybody react in a similar way to the same situation?
How can I learn the cues that precede a violent or negative or positive personal reaction?
What are the compelling factors behind the need to react?

Preceding Activities:

- The students listed five major cities and found the temperature of each in the newspaper.

- They located their city's temperature in degrees Fahrenheit.

- The students surfed the web to check the temperature for other parts of the world and created a compare and contrast temperature graph for five countries.

- The students kept a weekly record of the temperature each day for their city.

- Based on their log, they predicted the temperature for the next week.

Lesson Goals and Objectives:

1. The students become aware of their reactions to classroom situations and events and consider why they react as they do.
2. The students organize their reactions according to a temperature chart.
3. The students reflect on the classroom situations that incite personal reactions.
4. The students maintain a reflective journal.
5. The students make future choices based on increased self-awareness.

Activities/Assessment:

Warm-Up Activity: Group Activity. The students participate in a group activity with weather-designated cards (e.g., cloudy). They brainstorm and estimate temperatures for the kind of day described on their cards, and they describe things they might see, feel, or wear on the day indicated on their cards.

Hot and Cold Reaction Thermometer: Individual/Pair. Teacher passes out Post-it notes and a sheet with a list of 10 classroom situations that students encounter on a regular school day. Students write their reactions to the situations using action verbs. Teacher passes out an illustration of a thermometer that has six degrees marked on it—from extremely hot to freezing temperature. Students match the degree of temperature with their reactions to each of the 10 situations. They write down each temperature and the reactions that go with the temperature on a separate Post-it, then share the situation reactions and temperature matching with a peer. Based on their reactions and temperature matching, students create a personal hot and cold reaction thermometer using the 10 classroom situations. This is done on construction paper.

Temperature Designation: Whole-Class Activity. The teacher displays a large (3 feet or more) thermometer on the board with the six degrees listed on it. The teacher calls on students to stick their Post-its on the thermometer. The activity is followed by a general discussion on situations that match the extremely hot, hot, warm, cool, cold, and freezing temperatures. The teacher points out how self-awareness can lead not only to identifying reactions but also to some degree of control over personal reactions and also to a change in personal reactions.

Closure Activity: Journal Response. Students write a journal entry in response to the following prompts: "Am I aware of my hot and cold temperature reactions?" "To what extent can I control them?" "Why do I react the way I do?" "Why is it important to be self-aware?"

Follow-Up Activities:

Students maintain a personal temperature journal log with a reflection column for a month to document the situations outside of school that get them all worked up and heated or calmed down and cool, and they reflect on why they react as they do to these situations.

Students mime or dramatize temperature situations in groups, with emphasis on verbal and nonverbal cues that precede these situations.

Materials/Equipment:

- Classroom situations sheets
- Thermometer illustration sheets
- Weather-designated cards
- Master thermometer
- Post-it notes
- Journals
- Construction paper

Overall Evaluation:

Teacher checks student logs for organization (e.g., identification, dates for a month, situational entries, reflections).

Teacher observes for any increased self-awareness in students about their personal reactions over the targeted month.

Merged Teaching of Idea 5: Academic Content Standards Merged With Teaching Listening

Teachers' Names: John Doe, Pat Elachi
Lesson Title: Shakespeare's *Hamlet*

Date: Monday, March 4, 2004
Time: Morning English/social studies block
Grade Level: 12th

Student Status:

24 students: 15 females, 9 males (1 student is ESL); ability level within the class is consistent with the bell curve as shown from previous tests and activities

Overall Goal and Continuity:

The goal of this lesson is to help students interpret, learn, and relate to the works of William Shakespeare, specifically the play *Hamlet*. The students will continue their unit of study on British literature by studying the language and meaning of *Hamlet* and the cultures in which it was set and performed. We chose this lesson because we want our senior students' knowledge of British literature to include visualizing it and watching it on TV or stage. If the students can "see" *Hamlet*, while studying the script in class and for homework, they can feel more of a personal connection as well as continue to recognize the influences on American literature from British literature and history.

Instructional Purposes/Specific Objectives:

Objective 1—Students will continue to analyze the development of British literature, recognizing major literary forms and techniques, recognizing the characteristics of major chronological eras, and relating literary works and authors to major themes and issues of their eras (VA Standards of Learning 12.3 Reading/Literature).

Objective 2—Students will begin preparation for making and critiquing effectiveness of 5- to 10-minute formal oral presentations, including categories of audience, purpose, structure, support, content, and delivery (VA SOL 12.1 Oral Language).

Objective 3—Students will increase their awareness of the importance of listening and will practice with skills and procedures for effective listening (Idea 5; NBPTS Adolescence and Young Adulthood English Language Arts Standards, Standard X).

Content/Procedures/Activities:

1. A mini-quiz will be given at the start of class to see where students stand in terms of the assigned reading of *Hamlet* from their literature text. Those who are struggling or who have problems with the language (such as the ESL student) will meet with the teacher during the class work time. Those who finish early will be instructed to continue reading *Hamlet* in their texts. The quiz should not take more than 10 minutes for most students. The ESL student, if necessary, can complete the quiz in the back of the classroom. We will preview the day's agenda right after the mini-quiz.

2. The teacher will go line by line through especially difficult parts of the scene and explain what is going on while also mentioning different interpretations from critics of the play. The teacher will ask which interpretation(s) the students agree with but require them to defend their position. This is scheduled for about 30 minutes.

3. Students will view a short scene (15 minutes) of a current interpretation in class (e.g., Mel Gibson's *Hamlet*) and discuss differences between it and other interpretations, including theirs. They will also discuss the importance of emotions and actions of the characters that are expressed verbally in the scene.

4. The social studies teacher will give a brief presentation on the culture and times in which the play was set and written. Students will be asked to take notes on a distributed graphic organizer. Following this, the English teacher will talk about and demonstrate some examples of emotions "playing out" among characters, and then both teachers will invite students to take a role in a skit about the scene, in which they offer their version of Shakespeare's meaning and presentation. The skits will be prepared in today's work time and continued in the next class. (Also, in work time, students will begin thinking about an oral presentation—their own—which will be mentioned now and officially introduced later.) The drama skits will address the diversity of learning styles in the class, particularly

179

providing learning opportunities for those who are strong kinesthetic and verbal learners. (Research shows that lessons addressing a diverse student population are more effective than those that address a single learning style and do not take into account student differences.)

5. (Supervised work time—about 20 minutes; some skits will follow today, if time permits.)

6. Review will be conducted on the notes taken by the students, their recall of responses to the video shown in class, and their recollections of the emotions and actions verbally displayed before them by the teacher and the volunteer role-playing students. The accuracy or inaccuracy of listening will be highlighted, and students will see an overhead transparency on listening skills to further reinforce the importance of accurate listening as it relates to enjoying theater, effective and efficient note taking, and academic and personal success in school and in life.

7. Listening skill drills will be done in "helping trios," with one student practicing on another and the third student serving as an objective recorder. All three students will offer feedback to the practicing student on the teacher's signal. For the next round, roles will be reversed; three rounds will give each student the chance to practice the assigned skill and to receive feedback on his or her ability with the skill, including general feedback from the teachers at the end of each round. About 30 minutes will be needed for the drills, and if enough time is not available, the drills will be run tomorrow. The teachers will observe and listen to ensure our ESL student is comfortable in the drills and make appropriate modifications as necessary.

Materials and Equipment:

- Copies of the literature anthology

- Overhead projector and transparencies

- Sample (draft) rubrics for class

- Graphic organizer copies for class

- Sufficient copies of the mini-quiz
- Classroom dictionaries (for the ESL student)

Closure:

The class will be asked to share the "what," "how," and "why" of today's lesson. They will be officially assigned a 5- to 10-minute formal oral presentation on Shakespeare, his plays, *Hamlet*, or an item of historical/cultural context. The presentation will be due (TBA). The oral presentation will be evaluated by students according to a rubric to be agreed upon in class this week (sample distributed). One item of the rubric will connect listening done by the evaluating students to each individual presentation. Additional information on the oral presentation assignment will come tomorrow.

Evaluation and Follow-Up:

Students will be asked to turn in their lecture notes on their graphic organizers. (These will be checked and returned with comments.)

Students will be required to turn in a preliminary idea/outline for their oral presentation. This can be turned in today or during the week. It is, at this point, only a sketch of what students are planning, but it will help get the students organized for the assignment. The idea will be returned with suggestions from the teachers.

If scheduling permits, students, with proper permissions, will go on a field trip to the local Elden Street Theater to see *Hamlet* live on stage. The trip will be planned as a closing and culminating event in this unit of instruction.

Students will have the option for extra credit follow-up. This can challenge them and/or increase their overall grade. Their choice of extra credit assignment must be approved in advance by one of the teachers. An example is researching and writing a brief biography of their favorite British author or writing a synopsis of a most interesting (to them) period of British history (such as the one in which Shakespeare wrote *Hamlet*), with the reasons why they chose it.

Notes and Reflection:

This lesson is part of a required unit dealing with the development of British literature and literature of other cultures. As feasible, literature selections will include ones that can provide connections to the study of American and Virginia government, as well as shed light on the period of British history in which they were performed. Students in this class have shown a past tendency to listen effectively to one another in small group work, but not in whole-class discussions or teacher-led presentations. We, as the teachers, may need to reteach active listening skills, such as paraphrasing and summarizing, to the class, perhaps very soon. Interestingly, as teachers, we learned some things about our students in this lesson, such as Diane's reliance on one learning style and Khorsand's knowledge of British history, and we heard some interpretations of *Hamlet* that were unfamiliar to us—and made sense! Overall, it was an enjoyable lesson and we will continue with it tomorrow.

INTERSTATE NEW TEACHER ASSESSMENT AND SUPPORT CONSORTIUM (INTASC) MODEL STANDARDS FOR BEGINNING TEACHER LICENSING AND DEVELOPMENT

Principle #1: The teacher understands the central concepts, tools of inquiry, and structures of the discipline(s) he or she teaches and can create learning experiences that make these aspects of subject matter meaningful for students.

Knowledge

The teacher understands major concepts, assumptions, debates, processes of inquiry, and ways of knowing that are central to the discipline(s) s/he teaches.

The teacher understands how students' conceptual frameworks and their misconceptions for an area of knowledge can influence their learning.

The teacher can relate his/her disciplinary knowledge to other subject areas.

Dispositions

The teacher realizes that subject matter knowledge is not a fixed body of facts but is complex and ever-evolving. S/he seeks to keep abreast of new ideas and understandings in the field.

The teacher appreciates multiple perspectives and conveys to learners how knowledge is developed from the vantage point of the knower.

The teacher has enthusiasm for the discipline(s) s/he teaches and sees connections to everyday life.

The teacher is committed to continuous learning and engages in professional discourse about subject matter knowledge and children's learning of the discipline.

Performances

The teacher effectively uses multiple representations and explanations of disciplinary concepts that capture key ideas and link them to students' prior understandings.

The teacher can represent and use differing viewpoints, theories, "ways of knowing" and methods of inquiry in his/her teaching of subject matter concepts.

The teacher can evaluate teaching resources and curriculum materials for their comprehensiveness, accuracy, and usefulness for representing particular ideas and concepts.

The teacher engages students in generating knowledge and testing hypotheses according to the methods of inquiry and standards of evidence used in the discipline.

The teacher develops and uses curricula that encourage students to see, question, and interpret ideas from diverse perspectives.

The teacher can create interdisciplinary learning experiences that allow students to integrate knowledge, skills, and methods of inquiry from several subject areas.

Principle #2: The teacher understands how children learn and develop, and can provide learning opportunities that support their intellectual, social and personal development.

Knowledge

The teacher understands how learning occurs—how students construct knowledge, acquire skills, and develop habits of mind—and knows how to use instructional strategies that promote student learning.

The teacher understands that students' physical, social, emotional, moral and cognitive development influence learning and knows how to address these factors when making instructional decisions.

The teacher is aware of expected developmental progressions and ranges of individual variation within each domain (physical, social, emo-

tional, moral and cognitive), can identify levels of readiness in learning, and understands how development in any one domain may affect
performance in others.

Dispositions

The teacher appreciates individual variation within each area of development, shows respect for the diverse talents of all learners, and is committed to help them develop self-confidence and competence.

The teacher is disposed to use students' strengths as a basis for growth,
and their errors as an opportunity for learning.

Performances

The teacher assesses individual and group performance in order to design
instruction that meets learners' current needs in each domain (cognitive, social, emotional, moral, and physical) and that leads to the next
level of development.

The teacher stimulates student reflection on prior knowledge and links
new ideas to already familiar ideas, making connections to students'
experiences, providing opportunities for active engagement, manipu-
lation, and testing of ideas and materials, and encouraging students to
assume responsibility for shaping their learning tasks.

The teacher accesses students' thinking and experiences as a basis for
instructional activities by, for example, encouraging discussion, listening and responding to group interaction, and eliciting samples of student thinking orally and in writing.

*Principle #3: The teacher understands how students differ in their approaches
to learning and creates instructional opportunities that are adapted to diverse
learners.*

Knowledge

The teacher understands and can identify differences in approaches to
learning and performance, including different learning styles, multiple
intelligences, and performance modes, and can design instruction that
helps use students' strengths as the basis for growth.

The teacher knows about areas of exceptionality in learning—including learning disabilities, visual and perceptual difficulties, and special physical or mental challenges.

The teacher knows about the process of second language acquisition and about strategies to support the learning of students whose first language is not English.

The teacher understands how students' learning is influenced by individual experiences, talents, and prior learning, as well as language, culture, family and community values.

The teacher has a well-grounded framework for understanding cultural and community diversity and knows how to learn about and incorporate students' experiences, cultures, and community resources into instruction.

Dispositions

The teacher believes that all children can learn at high levels and persists in helping all children achieve success.

The teacher appreciates and values human diversity, shows respect for students' varied talents and perspectives, and is committed to the pursuit of "individually configured excellence."

The teacher respects students as individuals with differing personal and family backgrounds and various skills, talents, and interests.

The teacher is sensitive to community and cultural norms.

The teacher makes students feel valued for their potential as people, and helps them learn to value each other.

Performances

The teacher identifies and designs instruction appropriate to students' stages of development, learning styles, strengths, and needs.

The teacher uses teaching approaches that are sensitive to the multiple experiences of learners and that address different learning and performance modes.

The teacher makes appropriate provisions (in terms of time and circumstances for work, tasks assigned, communication and response modes) for individual students who have particular learning differences or needs.

The teacher can identify when and how to access appropriate services or resources to meet exceptional learning needs.

The teacher seeks to understand students' families, cultures, and communities, and uses this information as a basis for connecting instruction to students' experiences (e.g. drawing explicit connections between subject matter and community matters, making assignments that can be related to students' experiences and cultures).

The teacher brings multiple perspectives to the discussion of subject matter, including attention to students' personal, family, and community experiences and cultural norms.

The teacher creates a learning community in which individual differences are respected.

Principle #4: The teacher understands and uses a variety of instructional strategies to encourage students' development of critical thinking, problem solving, and performance skills.

Knowledge

The teacher understands the cognitive processes associated with various kinds of learning (e.g. critical and creative thinking, problem structuring and problem solving, invention, memorization and recall) and how these processes can be stimulated.

The teacher understands principles and techniques, along with advantages and limitations, associated with various instructional strategies (e.g. cooperative learning, direct instruction, discovery learning, whole group discussion, independent study, interdisciplinary instruction).

The teacher knows how to enhance learning through the use of a wide variety of materials as well as human and technological resources (e.g. computers, audio-visual technologies, videotapes and discs, local experts, primary documents and artifacts, texts, reference books, literature, and other print resources).

Dispositions

The teacher values the development of students' critical thinking, independent problem solving, and performance capabilities.

The teacher values flexibility and reciprocity in the teaching process as necessary for adapting instruction to student responses, ideas, and needs.

Performances

The teacher carefully evaluates how to achieve learning goals, choosing alternative teaching strategies and materials to achieve different instructional purposes and to meet student needs (e.g. developmental stages, prior knowledge, learning styles, and interests).

The teacher uses multiple teaching and learning strategies to engage students in active learning opportunities that promote the development of critical thinking, problem solving, and performance capabilities and that help students assume responsibility for identifying and using learning resources.

The teacher constantly monitors and adjusts strategies in response to learner feedback.

The teacher varies his or her role in the instructional process (e.g. instructor, facilitator, coach, audience) in relation to the content and purposes of instruction and the needs of students.

The teacher develops a variety of clear, accurate presentations and representations of concepts, using alternative explanations to assist students' understanding and presenting diverse perspectives to encourage critical thinking.

Principle #5: The teacher uses an understanding of individual and group motivation and behavior to create a learning environment that encourages positive social interaction, active engagement in learning, and self-motivation.

Knowledge

The teacher can use knowledge about human motivation and behavior drawn from the foundational sciences of psychology, anthropology, and sociology to develop strategies for organizing and supporting individual and group work.

The teacher understands how social groups function and influence people, and how people influence groups.

The teacher knows how to help people work productively and cooperatively with each other in complex social settings.

The teacher understands the principles of effective classroom management and can use a range of strategies to promote positive relationships, cooperation, and purposeful learning in the classroom.

The teacher recognizes factors and situations that are likely to promote or diminish intrinsic motivation, and knows how to help students become self-motivated.

Dispositions

The teacher takes responsibility for establishing a positive climate in the classroom and participates in maintaining such a climate in the school as whole.

The teacher understands how participation supports commitment, and is committed to the expression and use of democratic values in the classroom.

The teacher values the role of students in promoting each other's learning and recognizes the importance of peer relationships in establishing a climate of learning.

The teacher recognizes the value of intrinsic motivation to students' lifelong growth and learning.

The teacher is committed to the continuous development of individual students' abilities and considers how different motivational strategies are likely to encourage this development for each student.

Performances

The teacher creates a smoothly functioning learning community in which students assume responsibility for themselves and one another, participate in decision making, work collaboratively and independently, and engage in purposeful learning activities.

The teacher engages students in individual and cooperative learning activities that help them develop the motivation to achieve, by, for example, relating lessons to students' personal interests, allowing students to have choices in their learning, and leading students to ask questions and pursue problems that are meaningful to them.

The teacher organizes, allocates, and manages the resources of time, space, activities, and attention to provide active and equitable engagement of students in productive tasks.

The teacher maximizes the amount of class time spent in learning by creating expectations and processes for communication and behavior along with a physical setting conducive to classroom goals.

The teacher helps the group to develop shared values and expectations for student interactions, academic discussions, and individual and group responsibility that create a positive classroom climate of openness, mutual respect, support, and inquiry.

The teacher analyzes the classroom environment and makes decisions and adjustments to enhance social relationships, student motivation and engagement, and productive work.

The teacher organizes, prepares students for, and monitors independent and group work that allows for full and varied participation of all individuals.

Principle #6: The teacher uses knowledge of effective verbal, nonverbal, and media communication techniques to foster active inquiry, collaboration, and supportive interaction in the classroom.

Knowledge

The teacher understands communication theory, language development, and the role of language in learning.

The teacher understands how cultural and gender differences can affect communication in the classroom.

The teacher recognizes the importance of nonverbal as well as verbal communication.

The teacher knows about and can use effective verbal, nonverbal, and media communication techniques.

Dispositions

The teacher recognizes the power of language for fostering self-expression, identity development, and learning.

The teacher values many ways in which people seek to communicate and encourages many modes of communication in the classroom.

The teacher is a thoughtful and responsive listener.

The teacher appreciates the cultural dimensions of communication, responds appropriately, and seeks to foster culturally sensitive communication by and among all students in the class.

Performances

The teacher models effective communication strategies in conveying ideas and information and in asking questions (e.g. monitoring the effects of messages, restating ideas and drawing connections, using visual, aural, and kinesthetic cues, being sensitive to nonverbal cues given and received).

The teacher supports and expands learner expression in speaking, writing, and other media.

The teacher knows how to ask questions and stimulate discussion in different ways for particular purposes, for example, probing for learner understanding, helping students articulate their ideas and thinking processes, promoting risk-taking and problem-solving, facilitating factual recall, encouraging convergent and divergent thinking, stimulating curiosity, helping students to question.

The teacher communicates in ways that demonstrate sensitivity to cultural and gender differences (e.g. appropriate use of eye contact, interpretation of body language and verbal statements, acknowledgment of and responsiveness to different modes of communication and participation).

The teacher knows how to use a variety of media communication tools, including audio-visual aids and computers, to enrich learning opportunities.

Principle #7: The teacher plans instruction based upon knowledge of subject matter, students, the community, and curriculum goals.

Knowledge

The teacher understands learning theory, subject matter, curriculum development, and student development and knows how to use this knowledge in planning instruction to meet curriculum goals.

The teacher knows how to take contextual considerations (instructional materials, individual student interests, needs, and aptitudes, and community resources) into account in planning instruction that creates an effective bridge between curriculum goals and students' experiences.

The teacher knows when and how to adjust plans based on student responses and other contingencies.

Dispositions

The teacher values both long term and short term planning.

The teacher believes that plans must always be open to adjustment and revision based on student needs and changing circumstances.

The teacher values planning as a collegial activity.

Performances

As an individual and a member of a team, the teacher selects and creates learning experiences that are appropriate for curriculum goals, relevant to learners, and based upon principles of effective instruction (e.g. that activate students' prior knowledge, anticipate preconceptions, encourage exploration and problem-solving, and build new skills on those previously acquired).

The teacher plans for learning opportunities that recognize and address variation in learning styles and performance modes.

The teacher creates lessons and activities that operate at multiple levels to meet the developmental and individual needs of diverse learners and help each progress.

The teacher creates short-range and long-term plans that are linked to student needs and performance, and adapts the plans to ensure and capitalize on student progress and motivation.

The teacher responds to unanticipated sources of input, evaluates plans in relation to short- and long-range goals, and systematically adjusts plans to meet student needs and enhance learning.

Principle #8: The teacher understands and uses formal and informal assessment strategies to evaluate and ensure the continuous intellectual, social and physical development of the learner.

Knowledge

The teacher understands the characteristics, uses, advantages, and limitations of different types of assessments (e.g. criterion-referenced and norm-referenced instruments, traditional standardized and performance-based tests, observation systems, and assessments of student work) for evaluating how students learn, what they know and are able to do, and what kinds of experiences will support their further growth and development.

The teacher knows how to select, construct, and use assessment strategies and instruments appropriate to the learning outcomes being evaluated and to other diagnostic purposes.

The teacher understands measurement theory and assessment-related issues, such as validity, reliability, bias, and scoring concerns.

Dispositions

The teacher values ongoing assessment as essential to the instructional process and recognizes that many different assessment strategies, accurately and systematically used, are necessary for monitoring and promoting student learning.

The teacher is committed to using assessment to identify student strengths and promote student growth rather than to deny students access to learning opportunities.

Performances

The teacher appropriately uses a variety of formal and informal assessment techniques (e.g. observation, portfolios of student work, teacher-made tests, performance tasks, projects, student self-assessments, peer assessment, and standardized tests) to enhance her or his knowledge of learners, evaluate students' progress and performances, and modify teaching and learning strategies.

The teacher solicits and uses information about students' experiences, learning behavior, needs, and progress from parents, other colleagues, and the students themselves.

The teacher uses assessment strategies to involve learners in self-assessment activities, to help them become aware of their strengths and needs, and to encourage them to set personal goals for learning.

The teacher evaluates the effect of class activities on both individuals and the class as a whole, collecting information through observation of classroom interactions, questioning, and analysis of student work.

The teacher monitors his or her own teaching strategies and behavior in relation to student success, modifying plans and instructional approaches accordingly.

The teacher maintains useful records of student work and performance and can communicate student progress knowledgeably and responsibly, based on appropriate indicators, to students, parents, and other colleagues.

Principle #9: The teacher is a reflective practitioner who continually evaluates the effects of his/her choices and actions on others (students, parents, and other professionals in the learning community) and who actively seeks out opportunities to grow professionally.

Knowledge

The teacher understands methods of inquiry that provide him/her with a variety of self-assessment and problem-solving strategies for reflecting on his/her practice, its influences on students' growth and learning, and the complex interactions between them.

The teacher is aware of major areas of research on teaching and of resources available for professional learning (e.g. professional literature, colleagues, professional associations, professional development activities).

Dispositions

The teacher values critical thinking and self-directed learning as habits of mind.

The teacher is committed to reflection, assessment, and learning as an ongoing process.

The teacher is willing to give and receive help.

The teacher is committed to seeking out, developing, and continually refining practices that address the individual needs of students.

The teacher recognizes his/her professional responsibility for engaging in and supporting appropriate professional practices for self and colleagues.

Performances

The teacher uses classroom observation, information about students, and research as sources for evaluating the outcomes of teaching and learning and as a basis for experimenting with, reflecting on, and revising practice.

The teacher seeks out professional literature, colleagues, and other resources to support his/her own development as a learner and a teacher.

The teacher draws upon professional colleagues within the school and other professional arenas as supports for reflection, problem-solving and new ideas, actively sharing experiences and seeking and giving feedback.

Principle #10: The teacher fosters relationships with school colleagues, parents, and agencies in the larger community to support students' learning and well-being.

Knowledge

The teacher understands schools as organizations within the larger community context and understands the operations of the relevant aspects of the system(s) within which s/he works.

The teacher understands how factors in the students' environment outside of school (e.g. family circumstances, community environments, health and economic conditions) may influence students' life and learning.

The teacher understands and implements laws related to students' rights and teacher responsibilities (e.g. for equal education, appropriate education for handicapped students, confidentiality, privacy, appropriate treatment of students, reporting in situations related to possible child abuse).

Dispositions

The teacher values and appreciates the importance of all aspects of a child's experience.

The teacher is concerned about all aspects of a child's well-being (cognitive, emotional, social, and physical), and is alert to signs of difficulties.

The teacher is willing to consult with other adults regarding the education and well-being of his/her students.

The teacher respects the privacy of students and confidentiality of information.

The teacher is willing to work with other professionals to improve the overall learning environment for students.

Performances

The teacher participates in collegial activities designed to make the entire school a productive learning environment.

The teacher makes links with the learners' other environments on behalf of students, by consulting with parents, counselors, teachers of other classes and activities within the schools, and professionals in other community agencies.

The teacher can identify and use community resources to foster student learning.

The teacher establishes respectful and productive relationships with parents and guardians from diverse home and community situations, and seeks to develop cooperative partnerships in support of student learning and well being.

The teacher talks with and listens to the student, is sensitive and responsive to clues of distress, investigates situations, and seeks outside help as needed and appropriate to remedy problems.

The teacher acts as an advocate for students.

The Interstate New Teacher Assessment and Support Consortium (INTASC) standards were developed by the Council of Chief State School Officers (1992) and member states. Copies may be downloaded from the Council's website at http://www.ccsso.org.

REFERENCES

Agee, J. (2000). *A death in the family.* Thorndike, ME: Vintage International.

ASCD. (2003–2004). *Smart quotes.* Alexandria, VA: Association for Supervision and Curriculum Development.

ASCD. (2004). A healthy mind set: Coordinated efforts focus on the whole child. *Curriculum Update* (Winter),1.

Babbitt, N. (2000). *Tuck everlasting.* Englewood Cliffs, NJ: Prentice Hall.

Baer, J. (1997). *Creative teachers, creative students.* Boston: Allyn & Bacon.

Bayles, E. (1966). *Pragmatism in education.* New York: Harper & Row.

Bettelheim, B. (1976). *The uses of enchantment: The meaning and importance of fairy tales.* New York: Knopf.

Beyer, B. K. (1987). *Practical strategies for the teaching of thinking.* Boston: Allyn & Bacon.

Blanchard, K., & Johnson, S. (1982). *The one minute manager.* New York: Berkley.

Bowman, M. (Ed.). (1963). *Adventures in literature series.* Laureate Edition. New York: Harcourt, Brace & World.

Brooks, J., & Brooks, M. (1999). *In search of understanding: The case for constructivist classrooms.* Alexandria, VA: Association for Supervision and Curriculum Development.

Campbell, L., Campbell, B., & Dickinson, D. (1996). *Teaching & learning through multiple intelligences.* Needham Heights, MA: Allyn & Bacon.

Canfield, J., & Hansen, M. V. (Eds.). (1993). *Chicken soup for the soul.* Deerfield Beach, FL: Health Communications.

Canfield, J., & Wells, H. C. (1976). *100 ways to enhance self-concept in the classroom.* Englewood Cliffs, NJ: Prentice Hall.

Carr, J. F., & Harris, D. E. (2001). *Succeeding with standards: Linking curriculum, assessment, and action planning.* Alexandria, VA: Association for Supervision and Curriculum Development.

Castiglione, B. (1976). *The book of the courtier.* Penguin Books Ltd.

Charney, R. S. (2002). *Teaching children to care: Classroom management for ethical and academic growth, K–8.* Turner Falls, MA: Northeast Foundation for Children.

Clark, M. H. (1995). *Bad behavior.* New York: Harcourt.

REFERENCES

Clayton, M. K. (2001). *Classroom spaces that work*. Boston: Northeast Foundation for Children.

Connell, R. (2004). *The most dangerous game*. Whitefish, MI: Kessinger.

Council of Chief State School Officers. (1992). *Model standards for beginning teacher licensing, assessment, and development: A resource for state dialogue*. Washington, DC: Author. http://www.ccsso.org/content/pdfs/corestrd.pdf.

Dacey, J. S. (1989). *Fundamentals of creative thinking*. Lexington, MA: Heath.

Dennison, P. E., & Dennison, G. E. (1994). *Brain gym*. Ventura, CA: Edu-Kin-esthetics.

DeSpelder, L. A., & DeSpelder, S. (2004). *The last dance: Encountering death and dying*. Boston: McGraw-Hill.

DeVoto, B. (Ed.). (1953). *The journals of Lewis and Clark*. Boston: Houghton Mifflin.

DiCaprio, N. (1974). *Personality theories: Guide to living*. Philadelphia: W. B. Saunders.

Edmonds, R. (1979). Effective schools for the urban poor. *Educational Leadership, 27*(2), 23.

Fagen, S., & Long, N. (1976, October). On classroom discipline. *Instructor*.

Gardner, H., & Campbell, L. (1983). *Frames of mind: The theory of multiple intelligences*. New York: Basic Books.

Gazda, G. M., Asbury, F. S., Balzer, F. J., Childers, W. C., & Phelps, R. E. (1998). *Human relations development: A manual for educators*. Boston: Allyn & Bacon.

Goleman, D. (1995). *Emotional intelligence: Why it can matter more than IQ*. New York: Bantam.

Goodlad, J. (1986). *USOE secondary schools recognition program, 1983-1985. Educational leadership*. Alexandria, VA.: Association for Supervision and Curriculum Development.

Gordon, T. (1971). *Parent effectiveness training*. New York: Wyden.

Gordon, T. (1974). *T.E.T.: Teacher effectiveness training*. New York: Wyden.

Gray, J. (1992). *Men are from Mars, women are from Venus*. New York: Harper-Collins.

Guenther LeTendre, B., & Lipka, R. P. (2003). *Targeting violence in our schools*: *Thinking toward solutions*. Christopher-Gordon.

Hagen, P. T. (1999). *Guide to self-care: Answers to everyday health problems*. Rochester, MN: Mayo Clinic.

Hendricks, G., & Wills, R. (1975). *The centering book: Awareness activities for children, parents, and teachers*. Englewood Cliffs, NJ: Prentice-Hall.

Henry, O. (1994). *The best short stories of O. Henry*. New York: Random House.

Hillenbrand, L. (2002). *Seabiscuit: An American legend.* New York: Ballantine Books.

Jefferson, T. (1781). *Notes on the state of Virginia.* Reprinted in Lee, G. (Ed.). (1961). *Crusade against ignorance: Thomas Jefferson on education.* New York: Teachers College Press.

Johnson, A. P. (2000). *Up and out: Using creative and critical thinking skills to enhance learning.* Boston: Allyn & Bacon.

Johnson, D., & Johnson, F. (2000). *Joining together: Group theory and group skills.* Boston: Allyn & Bacon.

Joyce, B., & Weil, M., with Calhoun, E. (2000). *Models of teaching.* Needham Heights, MA: Allyn & Bacon.

Kubler Ross, E. (1997). *On death and dying.* New York: Simon & Schuster.

Lee, H. (2002). *To kill a mockingbird.* New York: Perennial Classics.

Lickona, T. (1991). *Educating for character: How our schools can teach respect and responsibility.* New York: Bantam.

Lindgren, A. (1977). *Pippi Longstocking.* Harmondsworth, Middlesex, England: Puffin Books.

Lindsay, V. The mouse that gnawed the oak-tree down. In G. Summerfield (Ed.), *Voices: An anthology of poems and pictures.* Chicago: Rand McNally.

Mehrabian, A. (1968). Communicating without words. *Psychology Today, 2,* 53–55.

Mourier, P., & Smith, M. (2001). *Conquering organizational change.* Atlanta, GA: CEP Press.

Napier, R., & Gershenfeld, M. (1993). *Groups: Theory and experience.* Boston: Houghton Mifflin.

Parks, G. (1987). *Learning tree.* New York: Ballantine Books.

Patros, P. G., & Shamoo, T. (1988). *Depression and suicide in children and adolescents: Prevention, intervention, and postvention.* Boston: Allyn & Bacon.

Percoco, J. A. (1998). *A passion for the past: Creative teaching of U.S. history.* Portsmouth, NH: Heinemann.

Poe, E. A. (1975). *Complete tales and poems of Edgar Allan Poe.* New York : Vintage Books.

Rigby, K. (2001). *Stop the bullying: A handbook for schools.* Portland, ME: Stenhouse.

Roethke, T. My papa's waltz. In G. Summerfield (Ed.), *Voices: An anthology of poems and pictures.* Chicago: Rand McNally.

Romero, M. (1997). *Roberto Clemente: Baseball hall of fame.* New York: Powerkids Press.

Sadker, M. P., & Sadker, D. M. (2005). *Teachers, schools, and society.* New York: McGraw-Hill.

REFERENCES

Saphier, J., & Gower, R. (1987). *The skillful teacher.* Carlisle, MA: Research for Better Teaching.

Schweitzer, A. (1990). *Out of my life & thought: An autobiography.* New York: Henry Holt.

Selye, H. (1974). *Stress without distress.* New York: New American Library.

Silverstein, S. (1974). *Where the sidewalk ends.* New York: Harper & Row.

Silverstein, S. (1999). *The giving tree.* New York: HarperCollins.

Smith, J. (2003). *Education and public health.* Alexandria, VA: Association for Supervision and Curriculum Development.

Sornson, R. (Ed.). (1996). *Teaching and joy.* Alexandria, VA: Association for Supervision and Curriculum Development.

Steinbeck, J. (2002). *Of mice and men.* New York: Penguin.

Stockton, F. The lady or the tiger. In M. Bowman (Ed.), *Adventures in literature series.* New York: Harcourt, Brace & World.

Thurber, J. (1994). *James Thurber: 92 stories.* New York: Random House.

Toynbee, A. J. (1972). *A study of history (1934–1967).* London, Oxford University Press.

Trelease, J. (2001). *The read-aloud handbook.* New York: Penguin.

Truman, M. Ordeal in the owyhee country. In M. Bowman (Ed.), *Adventures in literature series.* New York: Harcourt, Brace & World.

Twain, M. (1981). *The adventures of Huckleberry Finn.* New York: Bantam Classics.

Uchida, Y. (2004). *Journey to Topaz: A story of the Japanese-American evacuation.* Berkeley, CA: Heyday Books.

Van Dyke, H. (1996). *Story of the other wise man.* New York: Random House.

Wessler, S. L., & Preble, W. (2003). *The respectful school: How educators and students can conquer hate and harassment.* Alexandria, VA: ASCD.

Westbrook, R. (1991). *John Dewey and American democracy.* Ithaca, NY: Cornell University Press.

Whitebird, M. Ta-Na-E-Ka. In G. Summerfield (Ed.), *Voices: An anthology of poems and pictures.* Chicago: Rand McNally.

Wood, C. (1990). *Time to teach, time to learn.* Alexandria, VA: ASCD.

Wycoff, J. (1991). *Mindmapping: Your personal guide to exploring creativity and problem-solving.* New York: Berkley.

Yeats, W. B. Aedh wishes for the cloths of heaven. In R. Finneran (Ed.), *The collected poems of W. B. Yeats.* New York: MacMillan.

Young, D. (2004). Seeing beyond the averages. *Achiever, 3*(2), 2.

Zindel, P. (1974). *Let me hear you whisper: A play.* New York: HarperCollins.

Zindel, P. (1983). *The pigman.* New York: Bantam Books.

ABOUT THE AUTHORS

William R. Martin is a professor in the Graduate School of Education at George Mason University in Fairfax, Virginia, where he teaches introduction to teaching courses and supervises student teachers. Dr. Martin earned his bachelor's degree from Gettysburg College, his master's degree in education from Syracuse University, and his doctorate in English education from the University of Minnesota. With over 45 years of experience in teaching, including 9 years in middle school at Liverpool, New York, and the innovative University High School on the campus of the University of Minnesota, he has also served administrative roles in clinical supervision at the University of Minnesota, the University of Maryland, and George Mason University.

Dr. Martin has authored six books and numerous articles on teaching and has been a frequent presenter at local, regional, and national conferences on education. He lives in Fairfax, Virginia, with his wife, an attorney, and misses his three children, who have pursued their own professional careers in medicine and law. Dr. Martin enjoys travel, reading, and writing and is a daily tennis or swimming participant. He plans to conclude his professional life at George Mason University.

Arvinder K. Johri is a middle school English teacher with the Archdiocese of Washington, D.C. She has 3 years of experience at the middle school level and 5 years at the elementary level. She earned her master's degree in English literature from Delhi University, India, and her second postgraduate degree from George Mason University, Fairfax, Virginia. Ms. Johri received her teacher's licensure from GMU in 2003 and her M.Ed. in secondary education in 2004. Prior to joining the teaching profession, she worked for over eight years in the field of advertising, where she specialized in corporate copywriting.

Ms. Johri is currently a member of the leadership cadre for curriculum mapping in the Archdiocese of Washington and serves as a mentor for new teachers in the Archdiocese. She earned her Microsoft Certified Systems Engineer (MCSE) certification in 1999 and is one of three master technology teachers at her school. She has also spearheaded the ongoing character education program at Holy Redeemer Catholic in Washington, D.C., where she is a team leader for sixth, seventh, and eighth grades. In addition, she serves as the school coordinator for the Youth Crime Watch of America. Ms. Johri lives in Fairfax, Virginia, with her husband, a business analyst, and her school-age daughter and son. She continues to pursue her lifelong interest in writing poetry.